LAUGHTER!

Other Plays by Peter Barnes

The Ruling Class

**Leonardo's Last Supper
and Noonday Demons**

Lulu

The Bewitched

The Frontiers of Farce

LAUGHTER!

by

PETER BARNES

HEINEMANN
LONDON

Heinemann Educational Books Ltd
LONDON EDINBURGH MELBOURNE TORONTO
JOHANNESBURG NEW DELHI AUCKLAND
SINGAPORE HONG KONG NAIROBI
IBADAN KUALA LUMPUR KINGSTON

ISBN
0 435 23064 6

Published by
Heinemann Educational Books Ltd
48 Charles Street, London W1X 8AH
Set in 10/11pt Garamond by
Spectrum Typesetting, London
and printed in Great Britain by
Biddles of Guildford

TO MARTIN

CAST OF FIRST LONDON PRODUCTION

Laughter! was first presented at the Royal Court Theatre, London on 25 January 1978, with the following cast:

PART I

Ivan	Timothy West
Vaska Shibanov	Rodger Kemp
Tsarevitch	David Suchet
Semeon Bekbulatovitch	Barry Stanton
Samael	Derek Francis
Author	Rodger Kemp
Prince Nikita Odoevsky	Paul Bentall
Hammer	Stuart Rayner
Nail	Neil Borman
Axe	Patrick Connor
Tree	Patricia Leach

PART II

Viktor Cranach	Derek Francis
Hans Gottleb	Timothy West
Else Jost	Francis de la Tour
Heinz Stroop	Rodger Kemp
Georg Wochner	David Suchet
Abe Bimko	Derek Francis
Hyme Bieberstein	Timothy West
Gottleb's Mother	Patricia Leach
Sanitation Men	Stuart Rayner
	Neil Borman

Directed by Charles Marowitz
Designed by Pat Robertson
Lighting by Leonard Tucker
Costumes by Rosemary Vercoe

PART ONE

TSAR

Single Spot up, Down Stage Centre, on the immaculately dressed **Author** *with notes.*

Author: Ladies and Gentlemen . . .

A hand slaps a large custard pie straight in his face. As he wipes it off a laughing Voice declares: It's going to be that kind of a show, folks!

No it isn't. Gangrene has set in. Comedy itself is the enemy. Laughter only confuses and corrupts everything we try to say. It cures nothing except our consciences and so ends by making the nightmare worse. A sense of humour's no remedy for evil. Isn't that why the Devil's always smiling? The stupid're never truly laughed out of their stupidities, fools remain fools, the corrupt, violent and depraved remain corrupt, violent and depraved. Laughter's the ally of tyrants. It softens our hatred. An excuse to change nothing, for nothing needs changing when it's all a joke.

His bow tie whirls round and round; he angrily pulls it off.

So we must try and root out comedy, strangle mirth, let the heart pump sulphuric acid, not blood.

The carnation in his buttonhole squirts water; he tears it off desperately.

Root it out! The world grows hard, harder, and every time I open my mouth I subtract something from the sum of human knowledge. Laughter's too feeble a weapon against the barbarities of life. A balm for battles lost, standard equipment for the losing side; the powerful have no need of it. Wit's no answer to a homicidal maniac. So, in the face of Atilla the Hun, Ivan the Terrible, a Passendale or Auschwitz, what good is laughter?!

His trousers fall down to reveal spangled underpants.

Root it out! Root it out!

Spot out, and a magnificent Bass sings a Gregorian chant.

Lights up on the well of the courtyard of a Moscow chapel, 1575. The curved wall reaches up some seven feet and is only broken by a low archway Up Stage Centre. Above it is a figure of a Crucified Christ. Up Stage Right, **Prince Nikita Odoevsky,** *who is seated, impaled on a wooden stake. He* *wears a loincloth, his hands are bound, and heavy weights attached to his feet, so the sharpened point of the stake, which is covered with congealed blood like candle grease, is driven up through his body. There is an executioner's block, Stage Left.*

The cowled figure of **Abbot Ivan Moskovsky** *in the black monk's habit of the Russian Orthodox Church, enters quickly, bent low, through the archway. A large wooden cross hangs from his neck.*

The singing stops as he falls on his knees, Down Stage Centre, his prayer punctuated by **Odoevsky**'s *screams.*

Ivan (*blowing loudly*): Air, I confide my thoughts to you. Adam transgressed, Lot dissembled, Moses, Myriam, Aaron fell foul, Noah, David whored, sleered, craked in pain: 'I've sinned, wha' shouldst I do?' The Lord took away their sin. Mine rise Golgotha high: lust, greed, wrath, pride. Yet Christ crucified's a pledge o' God's pardon.

He crawls back to the crucifix Up Stage.

See, his hands nailed flat casn't strike me, feet hammered in, casn't run from me. See, his blood flows t' wash me, head down t' kiss me, arms wide t' clip me close. I play the bear, he gi's me honey; play Satan, he lights a candle. *Mercy's* the knife that turns, barb that bites. God wracks me raw wi' His mercy!

He bangs his forehead on the ground; it bleeds.

Red's the colour o' the Cross whereon God had a God killed. I came closest t' Him here, where men die, empierced, dis-soul-joined, new christianed in their gore. Clawed fingers grooved these stones, not penitential knees. Hot blood scalded 'em, not salt tears. List how the croked choir lilts full-voiced. Pain mined from the bone. *(he joins in the screaming) Uuuuuuuurrr aaarrr.* The Church must consecrate this molde, gar that block an altar, that stake an episcopal throne. F' only here canst the beshait sinner leally pray and suffer.

He rises and crosses to **Odoevsky**.

I betrayed our heavenly Tsar, you our earthly one. Your punishment's but a stake riven up through backarse cleavage where fartleberries cluster. Doest feel thy anus split, rectum

3

cleifed, pancreas lanced on a point, tripes born out in blood and piss-water? Then smile, your chastizer's human, not divine, who gi'es his victims, *mercy*. Smile, my son, that Christ stakes me not you! You buy forgiveness cheap. *Aaarrr*. I'm skolered in fire that burns wi'out light. Spiked not wi' soft wood but hot iron. He rives 't down through skullcase *crrack*. Brain-boiled gone, I stumble skirl-naked blind, amid its fell clouds. Torment scours you clean, turns me rancid. You go down purified, I putrify. My pain's infinite, yours has a stop. Oh, some men're lucky!

Odoevsky *(screaming)*: *Arrr-arrrrhh eeeee aaaa-aa hhhrrr.*

Ivan: 'Tis easy f' you t' say that but tisn't true. My pain's greater. We're apostates both but different in degree. You betrayed thy Sovereign, I my Saviour. We both sinned through pride, garled our leige lords, Judas-like. My sin's greater, therefore the pain. My examplar's Christ, yours only Muscovite Princes, whose tradition tis t' betray their annointed Tsar. Prince Garbaty-Skuisky beheaded, Prince Repin poignarded, Prince Kurlyatev strangled in a distant monastery. All f' treachery. Nothing else was e'er expected o' thee.

Odoevsky *(screaming)*: *Buuuuuuu ahhh rrreeeeee eeeggg aaaaa arrrrrkkkk.*

Ivan: Innocent? How canst say they were innocent o' all crimes? Why their very appearance constituted a criminal offence. You'd excuse Judas by saying he was hungry and needed the thirty pieces f' bread. Didst not the Tsar himself cry out in rage 'gainst 'em, *arrrrrgggrr?* Weren't they accused therefore guilty? Men can sink deeper, stay down longer, come up dirtier than any other o' God's creatures. Like swallows t' the sun they soar t' darkness. 'Tis why God punishes us.

Odoevsky *(screaming)*: *Uuuuuuu eeeeaaaaa ggg hhhh.*

Ivan: Meek? God's not meek. He peers into this world through our wounds.

Odoevsky *(screaming)*: *Mmmmmm arrrrxxx.*

Ivan: Good? Man's not good. He's a two-eyed, two-balled dawish freak who's seared soul's more foul than his sinsoiled carcass.

Odoevsky *(screaming)*: *Aaa eeee.*

Ivan: Deliverance? There's no deliverance. I asked God t' show me the way t' deliverance. 'How do I find myself?' I asked. 'Look under a stone' He replied. Root it out! Root it out! 'Show me the way t' deliverance' I asked again. He told me t' flee from men. Only when a sinner can crake, 'I and God alone're left in this world' will he find peace. Oh Lord let the alchemy o' my prayers distill this teeming world into a barren rock beneath a cold sun; empty the universe o' high stars, let black night come down.

The Lights dim to a single Spot on him.

Now mind casn't be soiled by human speech, body by human touch all senses pure, fountain-leap t' God. *(Odoevsky's screams fade)* Look on 't now. Gone. All sound and movement gone in darkness. Earth's made wondirly new, unslimed by men. Only in this well-willed solitude wi'out people t' dyke 't back canst my love flow free. Only in this new emptied planet canst I submit t' Thy will, Lord. Only here, alone, wi' a few simple tools — nails, hammer, axe, canst I raise a tabernacle t' Thy glory and find my true peace, *aaaarrr.*

He screams in terror as he sees in a Spot, Wings Left, a giant six-foot Nail with two legs, dashing in, pursued by a seven-foot Hammer. The terrified Ivan tries to scramble away but the demented Hammer gives chase and strikes him down, before vanishing into the darkness Up Stage after the Nail.

A Second Spot up immediately Wings Right as a seven-foot Tree rushes in chased by a giant Axe with legs. Seeing Ivan crouching in his Spot, Down Stage Left, the Axe attacks him viciously before racing after the frightened Tree and exiting in the darkness Up Stage. Gasping with terror, Ivan raises himself.

Ivan: The beams 're falling! Now *things* are in conspiracy 'gainst me. Objects show their natural hatred, a thousand doors open t' death. I'm surrounded by assassins! Knives leap at my back, stones cleif wide 'neath my feet, pillows press themselves down on my face, sleeptide. Sea, sky, earth all fellone nature's poised f' treachery. I'm Cain-marked! Who canst save me?!

A fanfare and Lights slowly up on Ivan crouching Down

Stage Left and **Odoevsky** *still impaled Stage Right as* **Tsar Semeon Bekbulatovich** *enters through the archway Up Stage Centre, wearing a stiff, richly embroidered robe, crown, heavy imperial collar and jewelled crucifix round his neck. He carries a long staff, surmounted by a gold globe and cross and tipped with an iron point as an unseen* **Herald** *intones:*

Herald's Voice: By the Almighty power o' God and the uncomprehensible Holy Trinity, bow heads f' Tsar Semeon Bekbulatovich, Emperor o' All Russia, Great Duke o' Volidemer, Muscovy and Novograde in the Nether Countries, Emperor o' Cassan and Astrachan, Lord o' Piskie and all the North Coast, Great Duke o' Smolenski, Tverski, Sibieriski and many others including Charnogoski, Rizariski and Volodski, in this the year o' Our Lord God 1572 ensuring.

Odoevsky *(screaming)*: Arrrrrhhh.

Ivan *(screaming)*: Arrrrrhhh.

Semeon *(screaming)*: Arrrrrhhh.

    Semeon *abruptly rushes Stage Left, falls on his knees and places his neck on the executioner's block.*

Lop. Jag. Strike. Disjoin this neck. Only rid me o' my cankered crown, if my head falls too what o' 't? Christ's crown o' thorns was goosefeathers compared t' mine. I want release. I betray myself. I wasn't garred t' command but obey, born t' nibble the earth not bestride 't. I'm one o' nature's natural crawlers. I long t' submit.

Ivan: Then submit t' thy haltane destiny o' being Tsar.

Semeon: I carry stones and on those stones more stones and on the topmost stone another pile o' stones.

Ivan: These're years o' triumph. Muscovy's brasted the Crimean Tartars i' the East and Sigsmund Augustus i' the West. Soon we'll secure Livonia, recover Kiev and the Ukraine and seize that longed-for gateway t' the Baltic Sea. We grow and the world trembles.

Semeon: Wi' laughter. I turn my back and they gwof 't behind white hands, smile in ounces. My crouching soul hears 'em tell the story o' how an empty carriage drove up t' the Great Palace and I stepped out.

Ivan *(pointing at* **Odoevsky**)*:* Laugh! Gowf 't I say.

    Odoevsky *groans.*

He doesn't laugh. He shakes and splits his sides but not wi' laughter. None gowf 't in God's presence, nor 'afore a Tsar who carries death i' his fingers.

Semeon *(taking off his crown)*: I'm not fitted t' rule, knees ache t' bend. Take my crown and I'll take thy place. I'm too dearch humble t' be a Tsar, you too prideful t' be a priest.

Ivan: I'll polt down my pride, swallow 't whole; till eyes no longer gauge the distance, mind no longer decides its lines. I strive t' join angelic hosts not sit cold-arsed on golden thrones.

    Semeon *thrusts the crown at him.*

Semeon: Let me be free! Take 't I say.

Ivan: Let me crawl t' salvation! Keep 't I beg.

    Still on his knees he backs away from the crown as **Semeon** *puts it on the executioner's block and pursues him frantically, also on his knees.*

Semeon: Only save me!

Ivan: Only let me be saved!

Odoevsky *(screaming): Uuuuuuuuhhrr eeee*

    Ivan *and* **Semeon** *stop their crawling and look up to see the bearded* **Vaska Shibanov** *who has just come in Up Stage Centre, staring down at them, dressed in long, fur-trimmed robes and carrying a sealed letter.* **Semeon** *pulls himself upright with the aid of his staff. He gestures with it to* **Shibanov,** *who opens the letter while* **Ivan** *remains kneeling.*

Shibanov: Sire, 'tis from the traitor-prince, Andrey Kurbsky o' Kurel. *(he reads)* 'Behold O Tsar. You call me traitor. Was King David such, forced by Saul's wrath t' flee and war 't 'gainst Judah? What gulf o' madness you plunge Holy Russia, what virtuous women defiled, drunken atrocities committed, loyal subjects lacerated wi' divers deaths wi'out justice or judgement . . .'

Ivan: *Arrrrgggrr.*

    He springs up with a cry of rage, tears off his heavy cross and hits **Semeon** *with it, sending him sprawling.*

Sonkar! Don't just stand there doe-eyed, pissin' milk! *(he grabs* **Semeon***'s staff)* You ha' authority's staff, cross and globe tipped wi' iron. Use 't. *Dramatize!* Dramatize so's men'll 'member your reply, not a traitor's curses. Words

7

fade, this never!

He brings down staff, spearing **Shibanov**'s *right foot to the floor.*

Again. Read 't again. This time wi' feeling.

He leans heavily on the staff as **Shibanov** *re-reads the letter, blood pouring from his foot. His voice is calm, but his body twists grotesquely in pain.*

Shibanov *(reads)*: 'Behold O Tsar. You call me traitor. Was King David such forced by Saul's wrath t' flee t' war 't 'gainst Judah? What gulf o' madness you plunge Holy Russia, what virtuous women defiled, drunken atrocities committed, loyal lacerated wi' divers deaths wi'out justice or judgement . . .'

Ivan *jabs the staff down harder.*

Ivan: Doest the iron bite 't? Doest the point impierce 't? Whose hand thrusts 't down? Who holes 't, spouts 't, garrs 't bleed?

Shibanov: You, Sire.

Ivan: Who am I?

Shibanov: Ivan Vasivitch, grandson o' Ivan the Great, son o' Elana Glinskaya and Vasily III, Emperor o' All the Russias — Tsar Ivan IV.

Ivan: Known as?

Shibanov: Ivan the Terrible.

Ivan *rips back his cowl and habit to reveal the familiar hook nose, long hair and beard. He snatches the letter, leaving the staff still spearing* **Shivanov**'s *foot to the floor.*

Ivan: I loved Kurbsky close. He fought at my side when I 'ssaulted Kazan's walls, hacked through its streets, clotted wi' Tartar dead. Yet he frighted, fled, foreswore, led foreign armies 'gainst me, God's anointed Tsar. Lucifer's stinkard! Let his tongue hang ripe. *(he reads)* '. . . women defiled . . . atrocities . . . subjects lacerated wi' divers deaths . . .' A sovereign casn't be judged 'cause he casn't recognise a superior: he's sovereign. Destroy me but never judge me, saying I caused divers deaths wi'out justice or judgement. *(he rushes to* **Odoevsky***)* Tell 'em how as Tsar I've slaughtered wi'out justice but never wi'out judgement.

Odoevsky *(screaming)*: Eeeeeeeee.

Ivan: There, Prince Odoevsky takes my point. I kill cold. A computed 120,000 grimed t' death, yold t' the sword. All were about t' betray me, there's nothing too cowardly f' 'em t' ha' the courage t' do. I knew their certain guilt by a certain sweating 'tween my fingers, *here, here.* I've never lacked judgement dealing final death, only wi' winning eternal life.

He crosses to **Semeon.**

I made you Tsar whilst I took the name Ivan Moskovsky and retired t' pray. F' two years I've monk'd 't humble, you've throned 't mightily. You've eaten o' the royal jelly — raise your hand Semeon, the ground slits, sky darkens. Yet still you've no meteors in you, no orbs, fire, bellows. The smiling babe smothers a bird i' its hand in joy at finding a creature weaker than itself. All men're born despots 'cept you. You've no taste for power. Tisn't natural!

Semeon *(rising):* Sire, you gave me staff, Monomachus's crown and the sacred name o' Tsar after the Assyrian and Babylonian kings, leaving thyself self-naked. Yet in peace and war governance is still thine. The Council o' the Zemsky Sorbor and Commanders o' your Armies still look t' thee f' orders.

Ivan: Despite my orders. I order 'em t' disobey me, 'tis the only order they disobey. Yet see how they'll jump t' swim seas o' vomit, wade nostril-deep through snot rivers, sleer wives and daughters, condemn their souls t' Hellpit on my orders. I gelt, spike, gut, serve 'em roasted and they still crake 'God save our one true Tsar!' as if ordered.

Odoevsky *(screaming feebly):* *Eeeeerrr rrrrrrhh uuuuuukkk.*

Ivan: Hear 't, 'tis the voice o' the people aching to obey.

Semeon: 'Cause they know my lion's skin's out at the elbows. Let me go back t' Tver and be crowned Tsar o' drunkards, eat sweetmeats on Sunday, catch sturgeon and beadle fish 'afore the rivers ice, sleep on my wife's belly, both eyes closed. I'll 've friends t' press about me daily there.

Ivan: Whilst here they only come close, the better t' cut throats at parting. Who? When? Where? How? This is centipede country. I don't ha' t' make myself understood, you ha' t' understand what I ha' t' say. *(to* **Shibanov***)* Why're you standing there watching?!

Shibanov: 'Cause my foot's pinned t' the floor, Sire.

Ivan: Oh that's glib. Why doesn't unpin thyself then, Master

Glib?

Shibanov: You've not given permission, Sire.

Ivan: Ah, glibber yet! *(he pulls* **Shibanov***'s beard)* Using the cloak o' obediency t' hide dumb insolence. Every breath you take's an insult 't God. I'll purge the air o' the air you breathe. Lies, ants' nests o' lies, rotting the fabric! No wonder I grow eccentric.

Shibanov: What can I do, Sire?

Ivan: 'Tis a question I've been asking myself f' years. *(he pushes the staff down harder)* Answer me this: I've tried t' un-Tsar my flesh, thrust my immortal soul at hazard, debauched, orgied, tyrannized, formed my dog-headed guards, my Opritchnina, and sleered whole populations at a whim, 1,500 an hour, women and children first: 'Follow me spare none!' Yet why doest still kneel and call this cruked carcass Tsar, Father o' All?

Shibanov: You're God's anointed. You've the authority o' blood, Sire, authority that rests on the past. It gi'es our world a permanence which men need, being the most unstable and futile creatures i' the Universe. You gi'e us certainty Sire, which is better than goodness.

Ivan A damn thinker! Am I t' be spared nothing?

Shibanov: 'Tis true, Sire, once I could define the true metaphysic as mastering reality and annihilating the phantoms engendered by brute superstition.

Ivan: Unintelligible solutions t' insoluble problems. Sapless talk.

Shibanov: But when I came t' court Sire, I bought pomade t' make my hair fall out, terrified I'd look too young and seem t' have ideas. F' I acknowledge there's no place f' philosophy or morality here, Sire, they're at best mere amusements t' divert a ruler's idle moments 'tween the business o' ruling. In truth, Aristotle played pimp at Alexander's court also.

Ivan: What good's Aristotle and his ilk t' me. He could only reason, I *know*.

Semeon: Then know, Sire, I long t' sink back into obscurity, pass into mist, melt 't wi' the mass o' men.

Ivan: I too thirst t' be unknown, steal out o' history, other men's dreams. They use me!

Semeon *(tearing off his clothes)*: I casn't wear these traps t' hide my covering o' worms. I'm the son o' Adam as Adam is o' dust. God's excrement. I'm miserable, damned, worse than damned — ordinary!

Ivan: Semeon, Semeon, love thyself. 'Tis the only affection you can rely on.

> **Semeon** *has taken off his shirt and breeches and stands forlornly in his dirty underwear.*

Semeon: Leuk, leuk. *(he slaps his face)* Wan-visaged, blubber-lipped. *(he slaps his stomach)* One bausey hanging gutsack. *(he slaps his arms)* And these arms. Can these spongy arms crest a world, these flabbed and farsey legs stride 't? Is this a body men bow to?

Ivan: They'll bow t' any crippled yole gi'en half the chance. All gods aren't Grecian.

> *He rips off his habit and stands in hairshirt and filthy loincloth.*

There's no bloom on my lyre, no summer left in me.

Semeon: But, Sire, you *loom*. Exposed t' the heights I shrink and tremble in the cold. *(he makes himself small)*

Ivan: Loom? *(he too makes himself small)* I'm God's flea, placed on Holy Russia's bovine hide t' sting and suck 't.

Semeon: Then I'm less: a flea's flea, the flea in the flea's gut, thy flea, Sire.

> *Both men are now crouching on their haunches.*

Ivan: I'll make th e swell. As the Lord said t' Peter; 'Arise, kill, eat' so fleas nee· bl od- neals.

> *F.e gestu·es and* **Semeon** *crosses with him, legs still bent, to* **Odoevsky**; *they crouch on either side of him.*

You'll ha' more than mere traps. I'll gi' you the power t' choose, t' judge when a man's ready f' judgement. Legs!

> *He takes hold of* **Odoevsky** *'s weighted right leg,* **Semeon** *his left.*

Now ring dem bells! I say ring dem bells!

> *They pull on* **Odoevsky** *'s legs. There is a great jangling of bells as the stake rips up into the victim's body and* **Ivan** *and* **Shibanov** *are spattered with blood.*

Odoevsky *(screaming)*: *Eeeeeeeeekkkk* God save the Tsar!

> *He slumps forward, dead.* **Ivan** *and* **Semeon** *straighten up.*

Ivan: Ah God was near us then. F' he's the author o' all punishment. Didst feel His presence? Didst feel His well-streams showering us wi' His grace?

He wipes the blood from his face and licks it off his fingers.
Taste the smart o' 't, Christ's precious blood, blessed Sacrament. I'll gi' thee the right t' play butcher, Semeon. Divide those t' be slaughtered from those fit f' breeding according t' age, weight and quality. T' choose those t' be hung on hooks, those t' end face down on a slab, quartered. I'll gi' thee the true authority o' death.

Semeon: I don't want 't, Sire, like quicksilver 'twill turn poison, card into my bones. I'd rather live pale, die trembling. Oh mother, mother take me back! Jus' gi' me peace, Sire, e'en if 'tis only a piece o' the grave. You canst ring my bells too, send me into that cold merk, at least there'll be friendly shadows there. Ring my bells, Sire, 'twill be a mercy. Ring 'em. Ring 'em. Ring dem bells.

As the Lights dim slowly, **Semeon** *seems to be pulled backwards across the stage.* **Ivan** *tenses, trying with a tremendous effort of will to force him to remain.*

Ivan: I casn't hold you. You've no love o' killing, no fear o' death. You slip . . . Your weakness too strong f' my strength. Stay. From heart-root I command. Stay. HOLD . . . HOLD.

But **Semeon** *is pulled back to be spread-eagled against a section of the courtyard wall Up Stage Left, which has turned spongy. He is remorselessly sucked into it and swallowed up, finally vanishing from sight. It is as if he had never been.*

The Lights have faded down to a Spot on **Ivan** *and* **Shibanov.**

Ivan: He's taken my salvation wi' him. I renounced my maggot-teeming acts o' will, brought obedience t' my soul. Now the panic world beats at my gate again.

Distant thunder of an approaching storm.

Gone the swallow's glide, yesterday's signs. *(he puts on* **Semeon**'s *coat)* I'm Prince of Destruction once more.

Repeated thunder as he paces round **Shibanov.**

I sleer men wi' fire from my third eye which cans't admit the light. Mind turns slow elipses i' the mire, open t' the night. 'T rhymes! 'T rhymes! Oh why doesn't life leave me alone?!

(he stops pacing) Why're you moving round in a circle like that?

Shibanov: My foot's still nailed t' the floor, Sire.

Ivan *(pulling out the staff)*: Must I do everything? Gi' me your report on my new system o' provincial Governors.

Shibanov: It has one defect Sire. Your Governors remain unpaid. Thus they're easily corrupted and hated f' 't.

Ivan: Good. Hatred's this world's fulcrum. It moves men more easily than luif or honour. Afore there was no appeal 'gainst a Governor's ordinances. Now the people canst come t' me f' redress. Leuk, now like a lodestone I draw in more polary power. 'Tis nature's iron law: those that have shall be gi'en. Power's sucked into this magnetized centre, where I stand.

He thrusts his staff into the air as a lightning conductor: a bolt of lightning strikes it and he judders violently: more follow and by their light we see **Odoevsky** *has now become a skeleton on the stake and* **Ivan** *and* **Shibanov** *visibly growing bent and old.*

In time I make all things flow t' the centre; all church property secularized; all army commissions sanctioned by me alone; all land registered so I know whose land t' take, whose t' add t'.

He passes a hand over his hair and beard: they turn grey.

Thus power converges t' a point behind my eyes. By laws magnetical. I've emptied the years.

The lightning fades away; Lights come up slowly.

And I'm left, soul skoldered black. I move little, else my body shatter into pieces and the lightning spill out. I am become a scourging rod, a roseless thorn.

Shibanov: No, you're the Breath o' our Nostrils, our Heart and Head, our Shorn Lamb.

Ivan: Truly is that truth? Real truth?

Shibanov: I canst only speak the Tsar's truth Sire, not real truth, truth's truth. Seneca spoke truth's truth and was razored f' 't; Socrates hemlocked. And they were o' the best. Matchless minds, bright intelligences grovel afore any dumb brute bringing slow death. I know I was once one o' that fair company. I had ethics.

Ivan: I don't care if you had carbuncles. Tell me truth's truth.

Shibanov: Sire, humanity can progress but I don't: I die.

Ivan: Prince Reprin once spake truth's truth t' my face.

Shibanov: I'd like t' meet him, Sire, and shake his hand.

Ivan: I'm not going t' the trouble o' having him dug up jus' so you canst shake his hand.

Shibanov: 'Tis true, Sire, truth must be buried grave-deep else we all wake naked from our dreams.

Ivan: No, I heard 't once years past, truth's truth, God's truth. When I was Abbot Ivan Moskovsky and Semeon Bekbulatovich was Tsar. I listened, God spake. I obeyed, God acted. All my wars were victorious then. I agonized o'er my sins but every day I knew the miracle o' Jesus walking on the waters as I walked through life wi'out drowning. Nothing buoys me up now. My wars turn t' defeats. My robes, my staff, age-old iniquities pull me low. I haven't even a gukkish, oyster-eyed Semeon t' take the burden. I crake again: "Who can save me?!"

Herald's Voice: By the Almighty power o' God and the Holy Trinity in this the year o' Our Lord 1581, bow heads f' the Tsarevitch, Ivan, Alexei, Kalita, Vasily, Mikhail, eldest son o' our Blessed Tsar, Ivan IV and sole heir t' the crown o' Monomach and all the lands and dignities o' the title o' Tsar.

Lights now full up as the **Tsarevitch** *enters, knocking against the archway Up Stage Centre in his bull-like rush. Dressed in bulky sable-trimmed top coat and shining boots, his gloved hands glitter with rings.* **Odoevsky**'s *skeleton gleams on the stake Stage Right, as the* **Tsarevitch** *pauses momentarily to stare at the* **Tsar**'s *crown on the execution block, before falling on one knee in front of* **Ivan**. *The* **Tsar** *gestures to him and he rises quickly.*

Tsarevitch: The Lithuanians besiege Pskov. Radzivill advances eastward t' the Volga. The Swedes 've taken Narva, Ivangorad, Koporie and Yam. The Poles under Stephan Batory demand the surrender o' the whole o' Livonia together wi' Sebezh and 400,000 crowns.

Ivan: *Arrrrggggrrrr (crying in rage he slams down his staff, pinning* **Shibanov**'s *left foot to the floor)* What didst he say?!

As **Ivan** *presses down on the staff,* **Shibanov** *again answers in a calm voice whilst his body jerks in pain and the*

Tsarevitch *strides about furiously, smashing holes in the wall with his fists.*

Shibanov: The Lithuanians besiege Pskov. Radzivill advances eastward t' the Volga. The Swedes 've taken Narva, Ivangorad, Koporie, and Yam. The Poles under Stephen Batory demand the surrender o' the whole o' Livonia together wi' Sebezh and 400,000 crowns.

Tsarevitch: Attack! Attack! When Batory first besieged Pskov I craked: 'Attack! Attack!' Sound drums, trumpets, scythe him wi' one blow.

Ivan: Ne'er risk all on a single battle. Thus Darius the Persian was destroyed at Arbela and Sinsharishkum the Assyrian at Nineveh, and their Empires down wi' them.

Tsarevitch: So you wait, wait, wait, wait.

Head down, he charges against the wall. Hitting it with a resounding thud, he merely lets out a short, stunned grunt, 'ugg'.

Ivan: Our commanders casn't be trusted. Prince Kurbsky and the rest betrayed us afore in the midst o' battle.

Tsarevitch: Then gi' me command. And I'll gi' thee back Narva, Ivangorad, Koporie and Yam. I'll gi' thee all Livonia and the Baltic seaboard you dream o'. I'll gi' thee victory.

Ivan: Or death. Ah my cluster-balled bull, carnage casn't be limited t' the common people. Canades and sharp steel're the only true levellers. They make blue blood spout as easily as red. I'll see you come back t' me on four men's shoulders: the dead commander o' a defeated army.

Tsarevitch: Or worse — the live commander o' a victorious one, ugg. *(he batters his head against the wall)* You fear my force, *ugg*. Steal my inheritance. Bury me deep. Crush the corn in the blade, *ugg*. All work against me!

Ivan: At your best son I'm better. But at times you remind me o' me when I was young. O' course you're not as suspicious as I was; not as devious, malignant, crabbyt. You don't inspire fear as I did. You haven't the ranclid cruelty I had or the forky strength t' eat, drink, lech or shit bricks like I used to. But in *some* ways you remind me o' me.

Tsarevitch: I want t' thrust. Let me thrust!

Ivan: I've made you sole heir and successor t' the whole. Left your younger brother Feodor, but fourteen towns. You've nothing to fear, 'tas been written down and witnessed.

Tsarevitch *(repeatedly throwing himself headfirst against the wall)*: Now, *ugg!* Now, *ugg!* Not later, *ugg!* I want 't now, *ugg!*

Ivan: Enjoy youth's last airy juices. Feel your testicles 're the sun and the moon whilst you still can. You're not ready t' take up the burden o' ruling. You'll find thyself chewing more than you've bitten off.

Tsarevitch: My neck-veins're hemp ropes. I paw the ground. Gore air. Shibanov confirm the truth, I'm ready.

Shibanov: You're ready, Sire.

Ivan: Shibanov confirm the truth, he's not.

Shibanov: He's not ready, Sire. Anyone who doesn't contradict himself's a dogmatist. Sires, I twist in the wind. You're my now and future Tsars. I can cringe, lick boots wi' a sycophant's rankling tongue and in extremis loose tiny, papier-mâché farts. But I casn't speak truth that's true f' you both. As a loyal, two-faced courtier Sires, I mustn't be pinned down.

Tsarevitch: Pinned? I'll ha' thee staked! I've been shaped t' rule. Schooled and groomed f' authority. Saw my first execution when I was three, handled the instruments o' justice, whips, brands, blocks, two years later. Sleered a traitor wi' my own hand when I was thirteen and slit open my close friend Vishavoty on mere suspicion on my coming o' age. You casn't say I'm not fitted t' take thy place, rule in God's name, not pity-purged.

Ivan: You're pity-purged but not passion-purged. There's too much anger in you, not 'nough hate. 'Tis a failing o' the young. Anger's a honey that soon loses its perfume, hate stinks forever.

Tsarevitch: I hate. F' love o' Christ I hate, *ugg. (he rams the wall with his head)* Heaven casn't contain my hate. Send f' the scalpers, *ugg!* I hate!

Ivan: Not 'nough t' sustain the terror needed t' root out disobedience. There canst be no rule wi'out terror. No opinion's innocent, therefore all opinions must be guilty. Like a steed wi'out a bridle so is a realm wi'out terror. The people hunger f' 't.

Tsarevitch: I carry 't in my hands. BOLTS. BOLTS.

Ivan: Not 'nough, son. 'Tis easy t' bring one man t' obedience, most're happiest on their knees. Some need only an imperious look t' kiss royal arses, others the symbols o' Cross and Crown, still others, authority's true reality — gnout and gallows. One man's trembling carcass's small but Holy Russia stretches from Smolensk t' beyond the River Ob, from Kola in the Arctic North down almost t' the Azovian Sea. T' bring this vastness t' obedience needs terror on an equal scale and I see no sign you're equal t' it yet.

Tsarevitch: Novogrod!

Shibanov (*imitating a funeral bell*): B-O-N-G...B-O-N-G...

Tsarevitch: I was wi' you at Novogrod.

Ivan: Their princes schemed t' betray me, join Kurbsky, found proof behind the ikon, Novogrod tholed like Moab like Babylon, the Lord said, 'Break their bones as the lion breaks the lambs, gar their skins black, skewer up their women, dash their babes 'gainst the stones o' Novogrod!'

Tsarevitch: So we sleered bloody every living thing *twang, swishh, urr.* Foxes, moles, lap-wings, bears.

Ivan: They wouldst've told Novogrod o' our coming.

Tsarevitch: And at the welcoming banquet men crouched outside wi' cleavers waiting f' your cry.

Ivan: *Arrrrggggrrr.*

He slowly falls on his knees.

Shibanov: B-O-N-G...B-O-N-G...

Tsarevitch: Then iron hooks pierced soft eyeballs, hot needles levered nails from broken fingers. Bellies slit wide, holes f' faces sticky round the edges and all this meat bleeding as the Priest called out the names o' the dead.

Shibanov *takes out a rolled parchment and chants a roll-call of the dead as* **Ivan** *lies spreadeagled on the ground. Rows of white cardboard faces appear above the wall: their childlike outlines are drawn in black with dots for eyes and downward curves for mouths.*

Shibanov (*chanting*): Remember Oh Lord the souls o' Thy servants o' Novogrod. Remember Pimen High Lord o'

17

Novogrod, known in this world as Procopy Cherny. Remember Kazarin and his two sons, Ishuk and Bogdan. Remember Bakhmet, Michael, Tryhon. Remember Sumork and his wife, Nechay and his wife, Nezhdan and his wife. Remember the twelve hundred members o' the Houses o' Ivanov and Staritsky whose names're known t' Thee Lord . . .

Tsarevitch: Remember those families flung o'er the Volkhov Bridge bound together so's not t' be parted e'en in death, and those that floated, piked, i' the river flooded wi' their blood.

Shibanov *(chanting)*: Their names're known t'Thee Oh Lord. Remember Prince Vladimir, Prince Nikita, Prince Boris. Remember the three thousand and eight clerks and the twenty thousand ordinary men whose names're known t' thee Oh Lord. Remember Oh Lord the souls o' sixty thousand o' thy servants who died afore their hour sounded in Novogrod . . .

Tsarevitch: Corpses stacked in piles, mounds of frozen entrails, charred torsos, splintered bones, heads blown open, brains out, pink hemispheres lying separate in the snow.

Ivan: We're all born t' live and die langsum, wake and sleep i' terror. The Golden Fleece they sing o' is a matted lump o' fur. Oh Lord I casn't think o' all the suffering in the world . . . so I don't.

He gets up briskly, the cardboard faces disappear from the top of the wall.

God sees no violent deaths. A steel blade 'cross a bare throat is jus' one more infirmity. 'Tis no worse t' end wi' a sword i' the intestines than a cancer growth; better the small dagger than the large goiter. What difference if sixty thousand die natural, scattered across the Urals in a day, or unnatural i' a city called Novogrod. We re-multiply. A quick thrust 'tween the shoulder blades takes us out, a quick thrust 'tween the thighs brings us in. All's in heavenly balance.

Tsarevitch: And I was not found wanting when I weighed in wi' thee at Novogrod. I learned there the scale o' terror needed t' rule an empire.

Ivan: But only through your eyes. I sucked terror warm from my mother's milk. My childhood days were strewned wi' knives. I was old very young. When Prince Shiusky ruled f' me as Regent he'd sprawl on the royal bed and spit pomegranate seeds into my face. God's chosen face! I quaked so, my breeches steamed. He couldst've poisoned me, sleered me bloody in some dark corner. But I survived. Made myself invisible, changed my shape like Volga Vseslavich. The country had no centre till I held and craked: 'Who'll kill him f' me?' They threw Shiusky t' the dogs but I'd known terror. 'Tis why I can use 't now, 'cause once my own bones melted; once I trembled.

Tsarevitch: Only once? I melt and tremble daily. I'm the son o' Ivan the Terrible.

Ivan: But you're my joy, my Easter bells, Anastasia's child, as sweet t' me as muscadin and eggs. Though six came after, your mother was my first and one true wife. She smiled roses. Then I never feared death only life wi'out her. 'Tis why we're closer yet than father and son. Oh how we've pranked 't, two young blades together. *(chuckling)* 'Member when our fool Dukuchay quipped 'In Holy Russia we never hang a man wi' a moustache. We use a rope.'

Tsarevitch: I poured hot soup on his head and you daggered him.

Ivan: And he fell flat as his joke. I was too rough, but he did once say that everything I touched turned t' rigor-mortis.

Tsarevitch *(laughing)*: And what o' that Festival o' St. Servius when you stripped a dozen court ladies bitch-naked and threw five bushel-loads o' peas at 'em.

Ivan *(laughing)*: Laugh, I thought I'd never dry my breeches. How their plump bubbies bobbed as they crawled round the floor picking 'em up. Oh what women we've shared boy, what strumpets, whores, two-roubled hacksters.

Tsarevitch: What lickerous-eyed plovers, what wagtails tripping 't soft.

Ivan: What trugs bearing their bellies out magestical.

Tsarevitch: What cheeks, what arses, shaming milk and cream.

Ivan: What legs and thighs shimmering as they danced.

    Ivan *and* **Tsarevitch** *stamp and clap rhythmically as they begin to dance 'The Cosaques'.*

Tsarevitch: Dance Shibanov. Are you ill?

Ivan: Don't stand there thinking — when a man's too dull t' dance he calls himself a thinker. Dance Shibanov! Dance!

Shibanov: I casn't, Sire, my foot's still pinned t' the floor.

Ivan: Oh glib! I've warned you afore about 't. Release thyself, and *dance!*

Shibanov *pulls out the staff and hobbles over to them. Accompanied by an unseen company clapping and stamping,* **Ivan** *and the* **Tsarevitch** *dance side by side, Cossack style, with legs bent and arms linked together. Quickly giving up trying to stamp his crippled feet,* **Shibanov** *whirls the staff round his head and leaps as they gather momentum.* **Ivan** *and the* **Tsarevitch** *jump and écarte with joyful cries. They spin round, always linked together, whilst* **Shibanov,** *using the staff for leverage, vaults high behind them. The stamping and clapping grows louder and faster as the dance reaches its climax with all three men soaring into the air with tremendous shouts.*

They finally collapse, exhausted. **Ivan** *and the* **Tsarevitch** *haul each other to their feet embracing and laughing.*

Ivan: My leming lufson boy. I leif you more than life.

Tsarevitch: Then let me swallow the sun. Yold the crown.

Ivan *takes his staff from* **Shibanov,** *who is hobbling about clutching first his right foot then his left.*

Ivan: It crushes. I'm crumped wi' power's pain.

Tsarevitch: T' please the poor, the rich say money doesn't bring happiness. Oh but it helps. It helps! T' please the powerless, the powerful say power doesn't bring joy. Oh but 't does. It does! Riding roughshod daily's the key to inner health. This world's a world o' power and those out o' power're out o' this world. Yold the crown.

Ivan: Sweet chuck, monsters thring in me. I thraward in merk. I suffer. Shibanov knows.

Shibanov: True you suffer, Sire.

Tsarevitch: You lie, your lips're moving!

Shibanov: True, you couldst say that too, Sire.

Ivan *(crossing quickly to skeleton)*: I suffer! Odoevsky knows. Tell 'em.

Odoevsky's Skeleton *(screaming)*: *Eeeeeeeee — aarrrrrhhh*

Ivan: They don't write songs like that anymore. *(he clutches his* *throat and struggles)* Root it out! . . . I've tried t' yold the crown but 't sticks like Nessor's shirt that sleered great Hercules. In 1543 I let my uncles Yuri and Michael Glimsky rule whilst I drank and hunted bear. They broke and betrayed me and Holy Russia. Then my tight-conscienced priest, Sylvester, ruled in my name. And when I lay baisted he too broke and betrayed me and Holy Russia. Adashev, Makary, Kuryatev, Basmanov, Bekbulatovich ruled f' me in their turn and turned wolsome in a day, whemmed and broke in a night.

Tsarevitch: 'Tis why you chose such hollow frekes. You gi' your power away only t' clip t' closer. You keep 't from me now, certain I'll ne'er break and gi' 't back.

Ivan: I keep it t' save you.

Tsarevitch: T' condemn me. You worship a God who had his only begot son ramed bloody.

Ivan: Out o' love.

Tsarevitch: Fathers must be eaten 'live by their sons. You keep 't from me out o' hatred.

Ivan: Out o' love, love.

Tsarevitch: You're a corpse, go be embalmed in Egypt. You keep 't from me out o' fear.

Ivan: Out o' love, love.

Tsarevitch: Out o' fear o' dying, old man.

Ivan: Love, love, *love!*

Tsarevitch: Mine, mine, *mine!*

He bends to snatch the crown from the block.

Ivan: *Arrrrrggghhh.*

Ivan hits him with the iron tip of the staff. As he falls, Ivan continues spearing him in rage.

Ivan: Love! Love! Only love!

The Tsarevitch crashes down and lies still. Shibanov approaches fearfully and bends down to examine him.

Ivan: Vérité, vérité Shibanov. Truth's true.

Shibanov: In truth Sire, though I've tried t' avoid 't all my life, now there's but one truth; truth's truth and Tsar truth merge. Your son's dead.

It begins to snow.

Ivan: Drown me, you tears. Suffering beyond the reach o' language. *KKK arrrxx ccrrrrr aaaaakk AAAARRR*

He sings the air 'Men Tiranne' from Gluck's 'Orfeo and Eurydice'.

'Men tiranne ah, voi sareste, al mio pianoto, al mio lamento, Se provaste un sol momento, Cosa sia languir d'amor, Se provaste un sol momento, Cosa sia languir d'amor Cosa sia languir d'amor.' Shibanov, conclude the peace treaty wi' the Polish Batory. We cede the whole o' Livonia together wi' Polotsk and Velizh but no compensation, no Esthonian ports and all Muscovite lands captured t' be restored. My dream o' a Baltic seaboard's lost. But we gain new conquered territory beyond the Urals. Send thanks t' our vassals, the Strogonovs f' the defeat o' the Siberian Khanate and capture o' his capital, Isker. Order Prince Bolkhovsky t' proceed there wi' five hundred men and receive the Tsardom o' Siberia on our behalf. Re-open trade negotiations wi' Elizabeth o' England and . . .

Lights Fade to a Spot on him in the snow as he sings the air 'Chiamo Il Mio Ben Cosi' from 'Orfeo and Eurydice'.

'Chiamo il mio ben cosi, Quando si monstra il di, Quando s'asconde Quando s'asconde. Ma, oh vano mio dolor; L'idolo del mio cor, Non mi risponde, Non mi risponde, No mi risponde!' I confessed t' the Council I cut the cedar, slew my heir. 'Choose another Tsar,' I craked. But they answered 'We want only you as our Tsar gi'en us by God.' So I cried out 'Holy Father, Lord God Almighty, I sleered my son!' 'Me too,' He answered, showing me his mercy, His terrible *mercy*. Who canst save me?!

Lights slowly up and we see the skeleton and the stake have gone but the crown on the executioner's block remains as a man emerges Up Stage Centre, out of the snow haze. He is dressed in a worn, double-breasted, blue serge suit, starched collar, waistcoat and stainless-steel framed spectacles. He crosses briskly to **Ivan** *and bows slightly.*

Samael: The name's Samael . . . Perhaps you know me better as Eden's Prince? The Angel who wrestled with Jacob at Penial, fetched Moses's soul? Ruler of the Fifth Heaven? Truth of the World? The Wind that Stinks?

Ivan: Who?

Samael: Death. Systemising Death.

Ivan: Death? Death?! But you're no carcass o' bones; you carry no scythe!

Samael: Bones're what I leave behind. *(he takes out a pocket mirror)* And this small mirror in which every man can see his own death's a better symbol than a scythe. It's true I used to mow down my harvest with that old-fashioned instrument and the phlegmatic calm of a peasant. But with the relentless progress of civilisation I've changed from being a stately angel to an over-worked head-clerk. Vultures can rest gorged on carrion. I can't.

Ivan: I don't believe you're Death. You've inkstained fingers, shiny breeches, frayed cuffs. You ride no pale horse.

Samael: I'm no longer significant enough for pale horses. I keep accounts, collect and record the depreciations and depletions in those worlds. Each super Nova and dying grain of sand is noted. Debit entries in the ledger, mathematical equations of pain and guilt, nets woven from accrued balances, plus and minus, red and black. In the end all accounts must be closed. It's a matter of good book-keeping; hygiene.

Ivan *(falling on his knees):* In nomine Patris et Filii et Spiritus Sanctu.

Samael: Imperatorem stantem mori oportet. 'An Emperor should die on his feet.' I appreciate you using a dead tongue but I prefer tomorrow's language today: non-operating deductions, contingent, liabilities, functional obsolescence. This is the end without sequel where everything stops. Give me the crown, then go fall into your grave.

Ivan: I casn't endure sunbeams, how canst I endure the brightness o' Him who made the sun? I'm not ready t' meet my God!

Samael: Which God's that? Each world has its Yaweths, Shang Tis, Amons, Ras, Indrass, its Creators, Judges, Joves, First-Movers, Bull-Roarers, Fathers of All. One sinks, another rises, the endless series cannot be told. They die too when space and time fade to shadow. Give me the crown.

Ivan *(scrambling up):* No 'tis my life.

Samael: That's why I want it.

Ivan: But I've been thy servant here on earth, as well as God's.

Samael: Naturally. We both wish to impose uniformity on all men, you of obedience, I of death. What sets worlds in motion, sends the green shoot thrusting, is the interplay of differences, their attraction and repulsion, sea-tide and heart-beat. We fight life together but you can hardly expect a special dispensation from nature for following your nature.

Ivan: But I've loaded your ledger wi' a computed 222,000 dead. That must be worth a week's reprieve, a day, an hour, a minute more! I'm too young t' die and too well-known.

Samael *(taking off his glasses and polishing them)*: You made death too personal, arbitrary, a matter of chance: too much like life. In the coming years they'll institutionalize it, take the passion out of killing, turn men into numbers and the slaughter'll be so vast no one mind'll grasp it, no heart'll break 'cause of it. Ah, what an age that'll be. How confidently they'll march on to extinction, not even a memory in the brain of the last crustacean crawling across the empty seas. Happy days. Happy days. Even Death has her dreams. *(he puts his glasses back and looks at his watch)* It's time for final audit. In real time you're in your bedchamber playing chess with Belsky. You take King pawn, I take your crown. End game. Account closed.

Ivan: I'll live through all eternity wi' a toothache only let me live!

Samael: Ivan, someday the day must come when the day won't.

Ivan: No. I cling! I cling!

Samael: Birds sit hushed before they fall, lilacs turn brown, men scream and run, believing an exception'll be made: 'Have mercy! Have mercy!' No class! You want to live forever?

Ivan: YES!

Samael: You can't avoid general deterioration of the total equipment. In time you're no longer economic to operate and you're written off.

Ivan: In spite o' death I'll fight!

Samael: It's every man's last privilege.

Ivan: But couldst I e'er win, subjugate Death as I subjugated men? Did Hercules wi' his strength? Ulysses wi' his wit? Cassus wi' his bags o' gold? Where's Xerxes? Tamberlaine's pomp? Hanno and Hannibal put down like dogs. Pompey's slit. Caesar hacked. Alexander dead. And I'm not feeling so good myself. *(he clutches his throat and struggles wildly)* Root it out! . . . Is't possible t' drive back the days of death again?

Samael: If you've strength enough and will.

Ivan *sticks his staff into the ground and they move apart.* **Samael** *removes his glasses,* **Ivan** *his robe, and both perform elaborate limbering-up exercises, lighten-fast punches and deep breathing. After stiff ceremonial bows, the two circle each other slowly. In the ensuing 'Kung Fu' style fight, amid savage punches and kicks, they never actually touch each other, though we hear the sound of their blows unnaturally loud.*

Ivan *finally catches* **Samael**'*s arm and sweeps his legs from under him. As* **Samael** *falls,* **Ivan** *snaps his arm and chops him savagely across the neck. There is a very loud 'Crack' and* **Samael** *lies still.* **Ivan** *stamps on him in triumph.*

Ivan: I've brasted the Eyeless Monster, slaughtered the Slaughterer o' Gods! *(he takes up his staff and puts on his robe)* Carnage maketh the man. I wax i' pride, wraith, cruelty. Retribution's devoid o' meaning. Here on the border of extinction I canst at last stand sham-less. *(he picks up the crown)* Truth's truth, I glory i' my crown. Oh how fine 'tis t' rule men, melt the stars in hot pride and wi' this staff pierce the side o' Him who made the world. If the Universe 'came a sea o' blood I'd prepare ship and sail her out afore I'd lose the title, TSAR. This's true catharsis, holy purging. Power's sweeter than wine, better than bread. F' truly, what shall 't profit a man if he shall gain his soul and lose the whole world?

He puts the crown on his head, the Lights dim down to a Spot on him.

Everything yields t' my will built upon the clenching hand, the stronger clenching fist. I casn't die, e'en if I die, f' e'en dead, men'll choose t' deck 'emselves in my dust, suck in my dust, eat my deadman's dust. I survive t' hold life in chains. No freedom, divine or human reigns. It rhymes, 't rhymes. I live! I live!

There is a faint crash in the darkness Up Stage and the sound of objects rolling across the floor. **Ivan** *goes rigid. A cry of 'The Tsar is dead' is heard, a funeral bell tolls and a sheet falls from the flies covering him as the Bass sings a funeral ode.*

The singing fades and **Ivan**'s *voice is heard over loud-speakers.*

Ivan's Voice: We dedicate this statue to the memory of Ivan IV, Tsar of Russia (1530-1584). By defeating the Tartars and conquering Kazan and Astrakhan, he brought a nation to birth. Out of the chaos of warring factions he created the first centralized, multi-national State in the West and proved an inspiration for those who followed. In his person he was like others, in his power, unique, the best educated, most hard-working ruler of his times. The title 'Terrible' was due to an unfortunate mistranslation; it was more accurately 'Ivan the Awe-Inspiring'. He was truly the father of his people, as God is truly the Father of us all.

The Russian National Anthem is played as the sheet is pulled up and away to reveal **Ivan** *in exactly the same position as before, leaning menacingly on his staff. But the Spot is now grey and his hands and face have turned the colour of stone: he has become a statue.*

Pigeons fly around him. As various National Anthems are played in quick succession, bird-droppings rain down in profusion, bespattering robes and crown.

The Spot slowly fades on the befouled figure of **Ivan** *to the strains of 'Deutschland Über Alles'. The Anthem continues blaring out of the darkness.*

END OF PART I

PART TWO

AUSCHWITZ

'Deutschland Über Alles' blares out briefly then fades. Lights up on an office in WVHA Department Amt C (Building) Oranienburg, Berlin, 1942. An eight-foot high filing unit stretches from Up Stage Centre to Up Stage Right. Its shelves are stuffed with grey files. Smaller filing units Stage Right and Left. There is a photograph of Adolf Hitler festooned with holly above the door Up Stage Left and a Nazi flag in a holder Up Stage Right. Nearby a small cupboard. The executioner's block remains Stage Left.

Viktor Cranach sits at his desk Down Stage Right, dictating a memo to **Fräulein Else Jost** whilst an elderly clerk, **Heinz Stroop**, replaces a file on the shelves Up Stage Right, and returns to his desk, which is next to **Fräulein Jost**'s Down Stage Left.

Cranach: WVHA Amt C1 (Building) to WVHA Amt D1/1. Your reference ADS/MNO our reference EZ/14/102/01. Copies WVHA Amt D IV/2, Amt D IV/4: RSHA OMIII: Reich Ministry PRV 24/6D. Component CP3(m) described in regulation E(5) serving as Class I or Class II appliances and so constructed as to comply with relevant requirements of regulations L2(4) and (6), L8 (4) and (7). Component CP3(m) shall comply with DS 4591/1942 for the purpose of regulation E(5) when not falling in with the definition of Class I and II. There shall be added after reference CP116 Part 2: 1941 the words 'as read with CP 116 Addendum 2: 1942 . . .' Six copies, Fräulein Jost. Despatch immediately. 'Will comply with requirements of regulations L2(4) and (6) L8(4) and (7)!' I don't mince words. I've always believed in calling a CF/83 a CF/83. How dare Amt D1/1 send me an unauthorized, unsigned KG70? Gottleb's trying to cut our throats behind our backs. He's out to destroy this department. *(he chuckles)* 'Component CP3(m) shall comply with DS 4591/1942 for the purposes of Regulation E(5)!' A *hit!* . . . A word with you, Fräulein. As civil servants we must be ready at any time to answer for our administrative actions. Actions based solely on past actions, precedents. Its therefore essential we keep accurate records. That's why everything has to be written down. It's the basis of our existence. Words on paper: Memo to Amt D III; memo to Sturmbannführer Burger, Amt D V etc. etc. Without them we can't function. They tell us what's been done, what we can do, what we have to do and what we are. The civilisation of the Third Reich'll be constructed from the surviving administrative records at Oranienburg, 1942 A.D. Unless of course they've the misfortune to dig up a memorandum of yours, Fräulein. *(he picks up a memo from his desk)* Will you please retype this. I know the first step's hard, but once you've tried it you'll enjoy using commas. Paper size A4 not A3 and the margins should be nine élite character spaces, seven pica on the left and six élite, five pica on the right.

Else: Naturally, Herr Cranach, if you look for mistakes you'll find them. *(she takes memo)* My OS 472 states I can do shorthand, typing and filing — but not all simultaneously. We're overworked and underfed. I can't keep Mother and me fit on a daily ration of a hundred and twelve grammes of meat, eight grammes of butter, forty of sugar and shop-signs saying: 'Wreathes and crosses — no potatoes.'

Cranach: Please, Fräulein! Remember, where there's a will there's a Gestapo.

Else: Coming to work this morning, I stopped to pull in my belt. Some idiot asked me what I was doing. I said, 'Having breakfast.'

Cranach: I hear they're experimenting with new dishes. Fried termites from the Upper Volga and grilled agoutis with green peppers.

Else: They can't be worse than those dehydrated soups. They actually clean the saucepans while they're cooking.

Cranach: It doesn't worry me too much. I've got worms and anything's good enough for them. I can recommend Dr. Schmidt's liver pills to alleviate any deficiency in your diet, Fräulein. They'll stop your hair from falling out too . . . Have you searched this morning yet?

Else *shakes her head and whilst* **Cranach** *continues talking, they all carefully search the office —* **Else** *and* **Stroop** *the filing shelves,* **Cranach** *round his desk.*

Everyone realises, Fräulein, our department has special problems. It's why Obergruppenführer Dr. Kammler had us upgraded and seconded from the Reich Ministry. We're now dealing with an estimated 74,000 administrative units in the three complexes in Upper Silesia alone, instead of 15,000 of just a year ago, and that's only the beginning. At the moment we still lack staff, equipment, space. You know I've been waiting two months for my own office, *ahh.*

He finds something stuck under his desk and pulls it out: it is a bugging device, attached to a flex; he barks into it.

And interdepartmental jealousies don't help!

He pulls the flex savagely and there is a faint cry of pain far off; without pausing, he takes a pair of clippers from his desk, neatly cuts the flex and puts the bugging device into his drawer.

As the first non-volunteers to work in WVHA, naturally Gottleb and Brigadeführer Glucks and the other hard-liners want us out. The knock in the night, the unexpected Foreign Service Allowance, the quick transfer to the Occupied Eastern Territories! *(they shudder)* We're under great pressure, but we'll triumph, just as our armies did last month at Stalingrad and El Alamein.

Stroop: Rissoles. Soya-bean rissoles with onion sauce à la Riefenstahl. I have 'em every day for lunch in the staff canteen, bon appétit. Very filling, Fräulein.

Else: I must try them.

Stroop: Early in the week.

Stroop sighs loudly. Cranach groans and Else sadly shakes her head. Stroop sighs, Cranach groans and Else shakes her head again.

Cranach: That's enough. We mustn't talk politics. It's too dangerous. Fräulein, bring me the material on the CP 3(m) tender.

They resume work. Stroop picks up two files with memos attached and takes them to Cranach, whilst Else crosses Up Stage to the files.

Stroop: What you just said, sir, about helping others, reminded me of Oberdienstleiter Brack.

He places the files in front of Cranach who glances at them. You remember Brack, sir. OMTC transferred to Resort K2 RMEUL. Big man, fat eyes, but made up for it with a bad cough. Almost as eloquent as you, sir, on the ideals of the service. Each man giving of his best, blending with the best other men give. His mind was such, I think, he could've been a world famous surgeon.

Cranach: I remember him. Tragic case. He always wanted to help suffering humanity but never had the necessary detachment. It must've been his experiences in the Great War; kept turning over corpses in his mind. I'm sure that's why when Bouhler set up the 'Foundation for Institutional Care' at T4, he applied for the post of Oberdienstleiter and became a member of the Party. *(he signs the two memos attached to the top of the files)* All those cretins, mongoloids, parapalytics, sclorotics and diarrectics — who doesn't want to root out pain? It's not true Goethe died peacefully, he screamed for three days and nights in fear of death. But there was no pain or fear at T4 under Brack, only five cc's of hydrocyanic acid. Incurables were finally cured. It was all repugnant to me on moral grounds, but I must say Brack always stressed the mercy in mercy-killing.

Else comes back with three files.

Else: Cardinal Galen denounced it from the pulpit. Only God can play God, make a tree, choose who lives, who dies. My mother would've been a beneficiary of Herr Brack's social surgery. It's true she's eighty-three and has developed whining into an art unsurpassed in Western Europe. But it's a sin to deprive the sinner of a last chance to reconcile herself to God.

Cranach: Public opinion was completely opposed to the euthanasia programme, even when Brack pointed out its benefits were only available to German-born nationals. The Führer — make-him-happy-he-deserves-it, had to drop the whole project. You see, despite what our enemies say, he can only govern with the consent of the German people.

He hands the files back to Stroop.

Stroop: It broke Herr Brack. He was prematurely retired on half-pay and a non-recurrent service gratuity. It could happen to any of us! You pull yourself up hand over hand but someone's always there with a knife, waiting to cut the rope. No one understands the arbitrary terror we all live under nowadays in the Third Reich — redundancy, compulsory retirement with loss of pension rights! *(he returns to his desk)* Today Herr Brack just sits in his room, unable to hear the word Madagascar without screaming.

Else: Requiescat in pace. Amen.

She has finished checking the files and puts them on **Cranach**'*s desk.*

The tenders for appliances CP3 (m). Krupps AG of Essen, Tesch and Stabenow of Hamburg and Degesch of Dessau.

Cranach *opens the files, whilst* **Else** *crosses Up Stage Right to the small cupboard to prepare coffee.*

Cranach: Herr Stroop, I'd like your opinion. Obergruppen-führer Dr. Kammler'll want the department's recommended choice. Krupps' DS 6/310 tender's a high 20,000 marks They claim lack of trained personnel on the site justifies pre mix concreting and the installation of chuting and pumping. I'm not prepared to encourage wild experiments in new building techniques at government expense. I favour Tesch and Stabenow.

Stroop: I agree, sir. They've proved most satisfactory. Amt D already've a contract with them for two tons of Kyklon B rat poison a month. Two tons. There can't be that many rats in the whole of Germany.

Cranach: Kyklon B isn't being used to kill rats but to discredit this department. *We* built those complexes in Upper Silesia. If Gottleb and Amt D prove they're overrun with vermin we're blamed. Q.E.D. Of course that's not Tesch and Stabenow's fault.

Stroop: I agree, sir.

Cranach: However, giving them another government contract so soon after the last might raise doubts as to our integrity.

Stroop: I agree, sir.

Cranach: Is there anything you don't agree with, Herr Stroop?

Stroop: Unemployment. I'm near retirement. You can't please everyone, so I find it best to keep pleasing my superiors. But I do wonder, sir, if it's wise to dismiss Krupps' tender? The firm's shown undeviating loyalty to the Party since '33. Old Gustav Krupps was awarded the War Cross of Merit and Young Alfred's Party number's a low 89627. They have influence.

Cranach: I'm not influenced by influence. Krupps've bad labour relations. They're only paying their foreign workers seventy pfennigs a day and refusing to build them a company brothel despite a UD 84763 directive.

    Else *puts a cup of coffee on his desk and one on* **Stroop's.**

In the old days, politicians were despised, administrators revered. Now politicians're sacrosanct and we've become the whipping boys of a public frustrated by wartime shortage and delays. They say we're divorced from the glorious reality of the National Socialist struggle. Our behaviour must therefore be seen to be above reproach. The final decision's the Obergruppenführer's but this department'll recommend Tesch and Stabenow for the CP3(m) contract. *(he drinks the coffee and grimaces)* I like my coffee weak but this is helpless.

Else: It's the new grain substitute. Secretly scented, *aromatically flavoured!* Unique — no coffee, all aroma. Wait till you try the new Führer-make-him-happy-he-deserves-it cigarettes. Filtered bootlaces. One puff, you're deaf . . . Two marks Herr Cranach. *(Cranach grunts)* For the bottle of schnapps Herr Wochner's bringing over. It's tradition to have a drink in the office on Christmas Eve.

Cranach: I don't approve, but as it's tradition.

    He opens a little purse, carefully takes out two marks and gives them to her.

Else: I know the Führer-make-him-happy-he-deserves-it has given the nation a new set of holy days to celebrate, like the 'National Day of Mourning' and the 'Anniversary of the Munich Putsch,' but they don't quite take the place of Christmas. Two marks, Herr Stroop.

Stroop: When she was alive my wife was so fat she never had a clear view of her feet. She loved food and jolly Christmases, cutting up apples, baking white bread, covering the fruit trees with a cloth. Good eating, drinking, sleeping, without 'em it's just staying on earth, not living. *(he gives* **Else** *the money)* Two marks for schnapps. Sixty for butter. Fifty percent on income tax, no lights in the street at night, no heating during the day. I'm spending this Christmas lying in bed holding a candle in my hands, staring at the folds and edges.

Else: I thought of praying to God at Midnight Mass for better times, but I know the Führer-make-him-happy-he-deserves-it doesn't like anyone going over his head.

Cranach: The State doesn't acknowledge God exists. If He did, I'm certain Adolf Hitler'd be notified before anyone else. Even so, concessions to Christ's birth've been made. Order 7334 Kd10 grants a Christmas present of one pair of stockings for every woman and one tie for every man over and above the rationed quota. Stockings for every woman, a cravat for every man. National Socialism works!

Stroop: But there'll be more black-edged Q4928's posted this year than Christmas presents. 'We regret to inform you your husband/brother/son/father has been killed in action defending the Fatherland.'

Cranach: The strain is beginning to tell. I see it daily in the 'Morganpost' obituary notices. The bereaved're no longer observing the Reichsinnenminister's Decree 77/B1 of 5th April '42 that all such notices must be a uniform, ninety-six millimetres broad and eighty long. But I've measured some of the latest obits and most're over *two hundred* millimetres long and *one hundred and twenty* broad! When my son was killed I could've written things. 'Fate has ended our waiting, our hope. We received the news our beloved son Joachim Cranach died from his wounds. All our joy buried in Russian earth . . . love him, mourn him, never forget . . . we live out the rest in grief . . .' and so on and so on. Instead I wrote, 'In proud sadness we learnt our son Joachim Cranach was killed in action in the East, liberating the Ukraine from the Ukrainians. Send no flowers.' That's under ninety-six millimetres broad, eighty long. Strictly in accordance with Decree 77/B1. What more to say. They pulled off his boots, dug a shallow grave and it was all over with.

Else: They're selling miniature hero-graves for four marks forty, at 'Kepa's', complete with tiny wreathes. Six for ten marks. Your wife might like one for her dressing table. *(she takes his empty cup)* Your son died at twenty-two, my mother lives, eighty-three and clinging fast.

She collects **Stroop's** *cup and takes them to the cupboard.*

34

All're dying, yet she survives with all the frail charm of an iron foundry.

Cranach *(opening a file)*: The German people've always preferred strong government to self-government. So why do they complain of too many decrees and regulations? It's one of the benefits of war. Usually our lives're so muddled that we don't know what we want, want what we don't want, don't want what we want. We're tormented by choice. Do you find it difficult to obey decrees and regulations, Fräulein?

Else *(putting dirty cups in the cupboard)*: No, fortunately I'm a Roman Catholic and Roman doctrine forbids any kind of dissent. Obedience is regarded as a principle of righteous conduct. So I look on National Socialism as Catholicism with the Christianity left out.

Cranach: We've had enough choices. We chose well because all choices're made for us. We've rules to live by which tell us what, when, where, how: no painful choices left to make except in sleep.

Stroop: German cheese gives me nightmares. I keep dreaming I'm punching Herr Gottleb in the face, though it's difficult from a kneeling position. The nightmares've got more frightening lately. I've started wanting to protest about conditions. I fight it but I can't resist. I must make my stand without the slightest 'but'. So I finally do it. I put a blank piece of paper into an envelope and send it to the Reich Führer himself. Afterwards I feel so proud! It's terrible. I wake up trembling with fright. I must stop sleeping with my eyes closed.

Cranach: You certainly can't afford to've nightmares Herr Stroop till you retire. You've taken a personal oath of loyalty to the Führer-make-him-happy-he-deserves-it. He'll know; he has devices . . .

He stops and sniffs suspiciously. **Else** *and* **Stroop** *are moving to the filing shelves, but he gestures to them to halt. The two watch him slowly rise and cross Up Stage, sniffing the air loudly. He pauses at the door for a moment, before flinging it open to catch* **Hans Gottleb,** *a chunky man with a Hitler moustache, crouching in the doorway, obviously listening at the keyhole.*

Gottleb, as I live and breathe!

Gottleb: Not for long if I can help it.

He straightens up and, gripping his briefcase, marches in, clicking his heels and jerking up his right arm in a Nazi salute.

Heil Hitler!

Else, Stroop *and* **Cranach** *raise their arms.*

Cranach:
Else: } Heil Hitler!
Stroop:

Else *and* **Stroop** *lower their arms but* **Cranach** *and* **Gottleb**, *facing each other, keep theirs stiffly raised;* **Cranach's** *arm is lower than* **Gottleb's**.

Gottleb: According to Hoflich of the 'Schwarzes Korps' it's customary when Heiling Hitler to raise the right arm at an angle so the palm of the hand is visible.

Cranach: Hoflich also wrote 'if one encounters a person socially inferior, when Heiling Hitler, then the right arm is raised only to eye-level, so the palm of the hand is hidden.'

Gottleb: Socially inferior! Why you sclerotic pen-pusher, my brother's a close friend of Julius Streicher, Gauleiter of Franken.

Cranach: Your sister too, I hear.

Gottleb: I warned Brigadeführer Glucks about you and your kind. He didn't listen. What gifts I've thrown before swine. You were seconded, didn't volunteer. Now you're a malignant virus in the healthy body of the SS — WVHA. You've no business here with your damn bureaucratic principles of promotion by merit and such. Merit, merit, I shit on *merit*. We old Party-men didn't fight in the streets, gutters filled with our dead, to build a world based on merit. What's merit got to do with it? We weren't appointed on merit. Take merit as a standard and we'll all be OUT.

Cranach: Gottleb, a man with a low forehead like yours has no right to criticise. Without more Upper Grade and Administrative Class officials who've risen on merit, Amt C & D'll collapse under the increased workload. 622.75 units per day're now being transported from all over Europe to Upper Silesia. We must've more trained civil servants to deal with 'em, not wild-eyed amateurs. Stand aside Gottleb and let us professionals do their job.

Gottleb: We scarred veterans're not going to be by-passed by you arse-licking, crypto-homo flunkies.

Else: Herr Gottleb, you haven't been reading 'Das Reich'. This is Politeness Month. Everyone has to help restore gladness, kindness and courtesy to the German scene. The Party's sponsoring a contest to find the politest men and women in Berlin. Dr. Goebbels himself's presenting prizes to the most successful.

Stroop: 'Even though you're German. / And it will come hard. / Just to learn to say you're sorry. / And win a week's supply of lard.' That won third Prize. Two theatre tickets to 'Sparrows in the Hand of God.'

Gottleb: Should be crushed. Like politeness. I shit on politeness. It stinks of philo-semite decadence, foul mind curves there. Let Judah perish! Politeness'll undermine our whole society. You can't give orders lisping, 'please', 'please', 'thank you' 'thank you' and the New Order's built on orders. Politeness is anti-German. Bluff rudeness, stimulating abuse, is the true Aryan way, hard in the bone. We must tear out from ourselves, the soft, the liquid noxious juices, *ahh*

He grunts with pain as he attempts to lower his stiff arm which, together with **Cranach**'s, *is still raised in a Nazi salute; whilst he pulls it down with his other hand,* **Cranach** *wincingly does the same before crossing to his desk.*

We didn't need politeness when we shot and clubbed our way through the beerhalls of Munich! Ah what days — sometimes I just want to be what I was, when I wanted to be what I am now. And we don't need politeness to crush the Bolshevik-Imperialistic half-breed armies in Asia and North Africa.

Else *and* **Stroop** *have resumed searching for files as* **Gottleb** *crosses to* **Cranach** *and takes out a document from his briefcase; he reads quickly.*

'All Section Heads WVHA (IV/QV) No. 44822/42 Ober-gruppenführer Pohhl. Further to the implementation of the executive solutions agreed at the Wannsee Conference Sec L (IV/QU) No. 37691/42 the attached document 'General

Instructions on Measures Sec. L(IV/QU)' is circulated herewith by hand and the signature of Department Heads is required on receipt of said copy.' *(He gives* **Cranach** *a form to sign)* You'll like paragraph fifteen, Cranach. Just your style. *(he opens the document at another page and reads)* 'Future cases of death shall be given consecutive Roman numbers with consecutive subsidiary Arabic numbers, so that the first case of death is numbered Roman numeral I/1, the second Roman numeral I/2 up to Roman numeral I/185. Thereafter cases of death shall be numbered Roman numeral II from Roman numeral II/1 to 185. Each new year will start with the Roman numeral I/1.' The dead talking to the dead. You bureaucratic tapeworms suck the colour from life. Our work here's a crusade or it's nothing. We need images of light to fire the mind, words to set the heart salmon-leaping. 'Stead we're given Roman numerals followed by consecutive subsidiary Arabic numerals, Roman numeral I/1 to Roman numeral I/185.

    Else *and* **Stroop** *join them with files.*

Cranach: This is war, Gottleb, a million words've died on us. We no longer believe in a secure sentence structure. Neutral symbols've become the safest means of communication. I certainly endorse the use of coded symbols rather than consecutive numbering in recording cases of death. It's more concise and less emotive.

Else: In any case, Amt D II/3 is Statistics and Auditing, Herr Gottleb. We're Amt C 1 — planning, costing and supervising of WVHA building projects.

Gottleb: Fräulein, you're a woman who could easily drive me to stop drinking.

Stroop: Deaths and paragraph fifteen isn't any of our business.

Gottleb: Ah, Stroop, still awake this late in the morning? Cranach, this office is only held together by the laws of inertia. Actually I've come over about the tenders for appliances CP 3(m) described in regulation E(5) Amt D wants the contract to be given to Krupps AG for past favours.

Cranach: Amt D wants? Amt D can continue to want. The contract'll be given strictly on merit. *Merit*, Gottleb, not on favours past, present or future.

Gottleb (*taking out a memo*): Confirmation of this request from Brigadeführer Glucks. Memo FC/867.

Cranach (*showing him a memo*): Amt C operates independent of Amt D. Obergruppenführer's memo JN 72.

Gottleb (*producing a second memo*): JN 72 or not. I've got a 62 KG!

Cranach (*flourishing a second memo*): And I've a 17Q!

Gottleb (*producing a third memo*): One 3H!

Cranach: Two spades.

Else: Four No-trumps.

Stroop: I pass.

All: Root it out!

> Cranach *waves* Stroop *and* Else *back to their desks.*

Cranach: There'll be no favours here. Thanks to favours received and given, bribery's become *the* organising principle of the Third Reich.

Gottleb: You elongated, bespectacled rodent. Without bribery you could never attract the better class of people into politics. Bribery's the reward for those who helped the cause and now need help. Bribery's the one expression of gratitude people appreciate. But you're one of those stiff-arsed moralists who see a favour as an opportunity to show their piss-green incorruptibility rather than their gratitude. Damnable petit-bourgeois morality. I shit on morality. It stiffens the brain, dries out life's juices. I've seen it ruin thousands of good men in my time: morality, virtue, boredom, syphilis. Downhill all the way. Corruption has more natural justice to it, not based on your shit-spat merit or morality. Anyone can take his share if he's strong or weak enough. It binds all men together. That's the National Socialist way. Nature's way. All things come to corruption, our bodies too: corruption.

Else: But 'this corruptible must put on incorruption and this mortal must put on immortality'. First Episode of Paul to the Corinthians.

Gottleb: No priest-talk Fräulein! Fat-gutted clowns with their mitres and jewels and their Holy Trinity of rent, interest and profit. You ask 'em to do something religious and they take a collection. Two thousand years they've been preaching love and charity and when a continent of corpses've shown how

39

bankrupt they are, some idiots still look at 'em and long for goodness. I shit on goodness! If there's a good God why is there old age and baldness, eh?

Cranach: God or no God, corruption turns the best to the worst. If I granted favours out of fear or greed, I'd betray my son charred black and the other dead who fell asleep twenty-two degrees centigrade below. I'd betray all those good Germans fighting from Benghazi to the Caucusus, so that the enslaved millions of Europe can be free.

Wochner: Heil Hitler!

No one has noticed **Georg Wochner**, *a young man in a long, weighed-down overcoat, slip in Up Stage Centre. All stand to attention and exchange Nazi salutes.*

All: Heil Hitler!

Wochner *(consulting a small note-book)*: Amt C 1 (Building) December 24th. Herr Cranach. One bottle of schnapps. Six marks.

He opens his coat to show the right hand side is lined with bottles; he removes one. As **Else** *gets the money,* **Stroop** *hastily resumes work at his desk and* **Cranach** *clears his throat.*

Gottleb: Count your days, Cranach! That's black-market schnapps. You're dealing in blacks. And I have witnesses. This room's wired. *(he shouts under the desk)* You hear that Winklemann? He's dealing in blacks! Blacks!

Cranach *takes out the 'bugging' device he cut off and silently hands it to* **Gottleb**, *who stares.*

Destroying government property too. That's a serious criminal offence, Cranach. You'll be cropped — CROPPED. Regulation 47632/48 imposes the same penalties on buyers as well as sellers of black goods. We've just slaughtered a Bavarian butcher found guilty of illegal slaughtering; hung his carcass up till it turned black as the rest of his meat. I'll see you all hung up turning black, black, black! *(chanting)* 'Oh let the blood spurt from the knife.'

Else *has paid* **Wochner**, *who unconcernedly ticks off the amount in his note-book.*

Wochner: Herr Gottleb, will you take your bottles now or should I deliver them to your office?

Gottleb: Give me two. You bring the rest. None of your dishwater bath-mix now.

    Gottleb *crosses as* **Wochner** *opens his coat again.*

Cranach: Leak into another universe, Gottleb! You're up to your armpits in blacks!

Gottleb: Don't compare your case of blacks with mine. You only buy schnapps to drink, I to relax tired bodies, tight minds. *(he gives* **Wochner** *money)* My men need compassionate leave, the same as other front-liners; I give it to 'em in a bottle.

Wochner: Five at six marks is thirty marks. Two marks short.

Gottleb *(giving him two more marks)*: I've been watching you, Wochner. *(he mimes counting banknotes)* Licking your forefinger and thumb flick-flick-flick-one-two-three-four-five. That's not the Aryan way of counting money. It's a sign of philo-Semite blood, counting money Panza-fast. Jew-blood, Jew-signs. Yes, their signs're everywhere if you've a nose for 'em. Biological proof of decadence. Prussian hair grows out spiky straight. But Czech moustaches all droop downwards. That's a sure sign they've got degenerate mongol blood. Stroop! Give your face a blank expression so I can tell you're not thinking! Why aren't you in the Army, Wochner?

Wochner: Just lucky, I have renal diabetes, cardiac murmur, crutch palsy, bat's wing lupus, Speighel hernia and Brigade-führer Glucks as an uncle. *(he gives two bottles to* **Gottleb***)* I'll leave the rest of your order in your office.

Cranach: This one still has work to do.

    He indicates the door, but **Wochner** *does not move.*

Else: Herr Cranach, it's customary to offer the black schnapps supplier a drink to toast the Fatherland and victory.

Gottleb: No one'll toast victory here, Wochner, even the women're defeatist to a man. They only drink for pleasure; patriotism's dead. Come with me and I'll show you patriotic drinking, gut-heaving, bladder-bursting drinking, real German drinking.

Cranach: As it's the custom. Herr Stroop, will you help Fräulein Jost with the bottle?

    Whilst **Else** *gets out the glasses from the cupboard,* **Stroop** *opens the schnapps.*

Wochner: Can I interest you in anything else? I carry a wide range of blacks from liberated capitals of Europe.

He opens his coat and takes various articles out of pockets on the left-hand side.

Silk scarves, Chanel perfume and toilet water, fifty marks. Fur muff, Paris label. Dutch butter. Pickled herrings from Warsaw, fifteen marks a jar.

He brings out a flat case filled with gold and diamond rings, which he opens concertina-fashion.

Something cheaper? Confiscated wedding rings. Gold. For you, thirteen marks, and I'm not making a pfennig profit. Twelve? Ten? Any offers? Here's a novelty that's selling well, very risqué. Hammer-and-sickle badges. Every one guaranteed taken by hand from the body of a dead Russian soldier. Look their blood's still on some of them.

Gottleb *examines a badge.*

There's a human tragedy in each one of those badges. I'm practically giving them away.

Cranach: Herr Wochner, this isn't an Afro-Oriental street market. Regulation AC 84/736(b) forbids these premises to be used for private business. Is this real silk?

He picks up a necktie as **Gottleb** *scratches the dry blood off a badge and tastes it on the tip of his tongue.*

Gottleb: Russian blood? This isn't Russian blood. I've tasted Russian blood. I know about blood. We've given the world the salvation of blood. And it sends us trinkets, beads, worthless trash.

He throws the badge back as **Stroop** *comes over with drinks for him and* **Cranach**. **Else** *serves* **Wochner**, *who has moved slightly to one side.*

Wochner: Fräulein, I'm looking for a wife — anybody's wife. What would it take to make you fall in love with me?

Else: A magician. My father said, work hard and be a good girl. You can always change your mind when you're older. Now I'm older and it's too late. I've reached the age where I'm beginning to find sex a pain in the arse.

Wochner: That means you're doing it the wrong way.

Cranach *(raising his glass)*: A toast. To the Fatherland and Victory.

All: The Fatherland and Victory!

They drink, stamp their right legs convulsively and gasp.

Wochner *(hoarsely)*: Good isn't it. Straight from the Hamburg boat.

Gottleb: Scraped off the sides. I can feel my toes exploding. Don't sip it like a virgin with lockjaw, Cranach. *(he mimes)* Drink it in one, head back, mouth open wide so it doesn't touch your teeth and dissolve the enamel.

He crosses and examines the bottle.

Smooth. But you've got it wrong again, Cranach. 'To the Fatherland and Victory' that's not a true National Socialist toast; the Gestapo could have a man's hanging testicles wired for less. I'll show you a true National Socialist toast. Listen. Learn.

Before **Cranach** *can stop him he fills his glass and raises it.*

A toast: to the Fatherland?

He drinks, stamps his leg convulsively and gasps.

Sm-o-o-th.

He immediately pours another glass and raises it.

A toast: Victory!

He drinks, stamps and gasps.

Sm-o-o-th. It's important to take your time, Cranach. Doesn't the Fatherland merit a full toast? Doesn't our victory?

Cranach: And doesn't he who is Victory itself? We've forgotten him. Let's drink to the man who made us what we are today.

Before **Gottleb** *can protest, he opens one of* **Gottleb**'s *bottles.*

I know you'll contribute to this dedication, Gottleb.

Gottleb *scowls as* **Cranach** *pours out the drinks.*

To the being who's given us a new centre of being, around whose head the cosmic forces gather into a swelling new order.

Stroop: Who loves us and forgives all that's weakly human in us.

Else: Who knows no sacrifice he would not let us make to be worthy of him.

Gottleb: Who has laid the axe to the sacred trees, told the whole world 'Step out of our sunlight.'

Wochner: Who turns the dross of pain into the gold of serenity.

They all turn to the portrait of Hitler above the entrace and raise their glasses.

All: The Führer — make-him-happy etc. etc.

They drink, stamp their right legs and gasp hoarsely.

Sm-o-o-th.

Singing the Wagnerian choral opening of 'Die Meistersinger von Nürnberg'.

'As our Saviour came to thee, willingly baptized to be. Yielded to the cross his breath, ransomed us from sin and death. May we too baptized be, worthy of his agony. Prophet, preacher, holy teacher. Send us by the hand, home to Jordan's strand.'

Cranach: Wrong again, Gottleb. No sacred trees're axed. On the contrary, their roots're watered, the status quo preserved. National Socialism is part of the great conservative tradition. It is based on solid middle-class values. Just as the Führer-make-him-happy etc. embodies our hopes for 'more' and our fear that when we get it, someone will try and take it away from us. Listen to him, speaking to the Reichstag 21st May '35. Noon. 'As National Socialists we are filled with admiration and respect for the great achievements of the past, not only in our own nation but far beyond it. We are happy to belong to the European community of culture which has inspired the modern world.'

Gottleb: Wrong again, Cranach. You only understood the words. But the sounds? What about the sounds?

He imitates the harsh nasal sound of Hitler's stabbing, lower middle-class, Austrian accent with its brutal, seductively hysterical, rhythms.

Szzztt nrrrr vrrr rrrchhhhh dddssss rrrrkkk rurrxxx ptsch nui KAAAA grrss iiiiichh R REECHTTT *RKK*!

A mighty chorus chants 'Sieg Heil! Sieg Heil!'

Rrrrrrrkkk hhhh dddttss vvllkkk rrrchh ... wrrrrkkk AAA! Ssrrt rrttt srrrr MPPFF gmuuuuttt cccHH dddrrr essskkkkk ZZZSWCH uuuuunn utt isssss KRR KRRKK SCHWEE SCHWRK SCHWRK sss uttu SCHWRK! SCHWRK! GROO SCHWRK!

All join in as the unseen audience roars 'Sieg Heil! Sieg Heil!'

Status quo, status quo, I shit on your status quo. Our world was dying of your status quo covered with status quo like horse mange. No air! No air! We flung the old order out of orbit, swept away the stiff-collars, monocles and cutaways, gave Germany social fluidity, permanent institutional anarchy. Before, our lives lacked the larger significance, he filled it with drama; there's always something happening in the Third Reich. He gave us faith in the sword, not in the Cross; that foul Semite-servility, that 'other-cheek' brigade with their 'Hit me!', 'Hit me!' Our hand goes out to all men, but always doubled up. You middle-class bed-wetters squeak about mercy, that's decadence; hardness, greater hardness!

Stroop: The truth is, as Jews can be simultaneously scum and dregs, so National Socialism can simultaneously embody revolutionary and conservative principles and black and white the same colour grey. That's the miracle of it.

He slumps into his chair.

Wochner: The true miracle is that a man with renal diabetes, cardiac murmur, crutch palsey, bat's wing lupus and Spieghel hernia can prosper, not despite his afflictions but because of 'em. And I want to see another miracle, when this country's business'll only be business. Nothing'll stop us then, we'll be the paymasters of Europe. It'll be easy. No more uncertainties, we'll be able to judge a man's worth at a glance by his credit rating, know right from wrong, success from failure, by the amount of money in our pockets. Money's a necessity I've always placed just ahead of breathing.

Cranach: Wochner, I shall ignore you with every fibre of my being. We Germans've always had the divine capacity for visions which transcended the merely commercial. That's why the Reichführer S.S. Heinrich Himmler himself, decreed that our first complex should be built in the forest outside Weimar, the very seat of German classical tradition. Didn't he leave Goethe's famous oak tree standing there in the middle of the compound and constructed the ramps, and block houses around it? You see, even in times like these, in places like that, for people like them, German culture is made available to all. We think transcendentally. We raise our eyes to the hills; the soul, the soul, the German soul! And you talk of money, credit ratings.

Gottleb: Materialistic filth! People spending money they haven't earned, to buy things they don't need, to impress neighbours who don't care. In the old days Wochner we'd've washed your mouth out with prussic acid. Our nation'll never descend to prosperity. I shit on prosperity. Hideous self-sacrifice is our way of life. You know nothing of sacrifice or suffering Wochner. What with renal diabetes, cardiac murmur, crutch palsey, bat's wing lupus and Spieghel hernia, you've had it too soft. Soft! Herr Cranach is right. You can only be ignored. *(he takes another drink)* After a time this stuff grows on you, like leaf mould. Herr Cranach, I think we should examine memos FC/867, 62KG and 3H regarding CP3(m). If you're agreeable that is?

Cranach *nods, crosses and sits at his desk.* **Gottleb** *stands beside him. They examine the papers together and drink their schnapps.* **Wochner** *shrugs and starts putting the goods back into his coat with* **Else**'*s help.*

Wochner: My fairest lady, may I offer you my arm and company tonight?

Else: I'm not fair, no lady, and I don't need an escort to see me home. I know men, when they're soft they're hard, when they're hard they're soft. I expect nothing from 'em, and that's what I always get — nothing. One of my fiancés once bought me a beautiful ring with a place for a lovely diamond in it.

Wochner: I had a fiancée but we broke it off on religious grounds. I worshipped money and she didn't have any.

Else: I've heard of your effect on women. Just being near you gives a girl hives.

Wochner: Women always judge with their bodies instead of their minds. I'll come for you tonight.

Else: 'I'll come for you tonight.' Act like a lover if you want to be one. Tell me, 'the brightness of your cheek outshines the stars, one glance from your eyes outweighs the wisdom of the world.' Woo me, say something beautiful.

Wochner: One jar of Kiel salt herrings. Two kilos of real coffee, four fresh eggs. One tin of skimmed milk.

46

Else: The answer's no. No. No. No.

Wochner: Three kilos of butter. Six of lard. One real woollen blanket. Three kilos of bacon.

Else *(quickly)*: Three kilos of bacon plus the woollen blanket!

Wochner: I had Herr Sauckel's wife for three kilos of bacon. If I'd thrown in a wollen blanket I'd've got Herr Sauckel too. Only promise you won't talk of love while we make it. I desire you, enjoy you, utilize you. Love doesn't come into it. *(he takes her hand)* I kiss your hand.

Else: Tonight it'll be all over, fortunately. Bring the goods with you or it's no trade.

> **Wochner** *nods and turns to the others.*

Wochner: Gentlemen, I have to go.

Cranach: In the end haven't we all.

> **Wochner** *bows slightly and exits, his coat still weighing him down.* **Else** *pours herself another drink.*

Stroop: There were always as many women available when I was young as there are now. But what I hate about life is there's always a new lot enjoying 'em. There's nothing sadder than an old roué with nothing left to rue.

Cranach: Was Wochner ever in the Hitler Youth? — tough as leather, swift as whippets, hard as Krupp steel. Somehow I can't see him sitting round a camp-fire singing the Horst Wessel Song and dreaming of being a Gauleiter like any normal German boy.

Gottleb: Wochner's time's short. Brigadeführer Glucks won't be able to save him. I've seen to it. Certain Party officials know about his filthy Empire of blacks — and they want their share. Any moment now that tide-mark won't be the only thing around his neck.

Else: Please, not until after I've finished my business with him, Herr Gottleb.

Gottleb *(he opens his other bottle)*: To please you Fräulein, I'll let him enjoy Christmas. It never hurts to show a little compassion and warm the knife before you stick it in. *(he pours her another drink)* This schnapps must be stronger than I thought. You're beginning to look attractive, Fräulein, in an elementary sort of way. Why aren't you married? The Führer-make-him-happy etc. promised every woman in the

Third Reich a husband, dead or alive. A woman should be in her own home, behind a spinning wheel, weaving heavenly roses.

Else: The whole of Germany is our home and we must serve her wherever we can.

Gottleb: And you've no children. We must all do our part for the perpetuation of the Nordic race. I've been a virile lover, thirty years, man and boy. The boy's worn out, but the man's still active.

Else: I've tried, but Karl was killed in Norway, Horst in the Belgian Ardennes, Kurt and Josef taken in the taking of Greece and Crete, Fritz assaulting Tobruk, Edgar capturing Kiev. All great victories, but death didn't seem to know that, made no distinction pro or contra. Left me standing at the altar whilst my mother survived.

Cranach: You could still have had children without benefit of. And no stigma. Reichsminister Lammers' ruling, memo QBX 54738 that extra-marital motherhood was not a reason for initiating disciplinary measures against female members of the civil service.

Gottleb: We've replaced hypocritical bourgeois morality with honest National Socialist immorality.

Else: Venereal satisfaction outside wedlock's a mortal sin, unless forced and without pleasure. I can't commit mortal sin, cut myself off from God's light, grace, my last end.

Gottleb: Jew talk! You've a good child-bearing pelvis, Fräulein. But just look at yourself. I know the Party's ideal woman is one of Spartan severity, but you go too far. Without those glasses, that hair-style, why you'd be beautiful. Here, let me show you.

He takes off her glasses, then removes the comb keeping her bun in place.

Don't worry, I've got very delicate hands . . . Just let it fall out . . .

Else's *hair tumbles down, she shakes it free.*

There, there, you see, Fräulein . . . why you look . . .

She glances up; he shudders.

worse!

Else *grabs the comb and starts putting her hair back up.*

Else: If we're ever alone on a desert island, Herr Gottleb, bring a pack of cards.

Stroop: When we were kids, we used to take a stick and hit each other over the head. Even the games were different then. I liked to be domineering, but I could never find anyone who wanted to be submissive.

Else has fixed her hair back into a bun and puts her glasses on. Gottleb points triumphantly.

Gottleb: There, I was right. The hair, the glasses, it makes all the difference. Why, now you look almost beautiful, Fräulein Jost.

Else: But this is exactly the way I was before!

Gottleb: And not a moment too soon.

Cranach stands up, sways slightly, and sits again. All are getting progressively more drunk.

Cranach: Gottleb, I've studied these memos and I still can't grant special favours to Krupps AG.

Gottleb: I understand perfectly Cranach. I don't agree with what you say and I'll fight to death your right to say it. I can't be fairer than that. Have another drink.

He pours himself and Cranach another drink.

Cranach: I don't want to be unfair, Gottleb. If you wish the Reichführer S.S. Heinrich Himmler himself to renew the case I'd've no objection.

Gottleb: Ah, the Reichführer's a truly great man, trying to recreate the pure Aryan race according to Mendel's laws. His commitment to the community's total, TOTAL. 'If ten thousand Russian women die digging a tank ditch, it interests me only as far as the tank ditch is completed for Germany.'

Cranach: But he also said, 'We Germans're the only people with a decent attitude to animals.' I don't understand why he has such a bad reputation.

Gottleb: I met him once in person. He was sitting at a large black table with a bottle of mineral water and Obergruppen-führers Jeckeln, Kaltenbrunner and von Herff. They were all staring into space, forcing a traitor in the next room to confess, purely by exerting their collective Aryan wills. It was called an exercise in concentration. Of course the SS're usually more physical in their approach. But this time they were dealing with a cross-eyed, bearded dwarf.

Cranach: An intellectual?

Gottleb: Yes, the subtle method can sometimes be very effective with intellectuals. Of course if they turn out not to be intellectuals, you can always go back to basics; put the needle in the record and separate the soul from the wax with traditional whips, cold chisels and such.

Else: Tell me, do fully uniformed men actually believe they can force someone to tell them the truth by will power alone?

Gottleb: If the will's truly Aryan. Aryan will cuts through steel plate, thirty metres thick. It's pure light, burning light. I'll show you. You've no intellectuals here, so we'll have to use old Stroop — there's a full moon tonight but it won't make him any brighter. Right, Stroop?

> **Stroop,** *slumped in his chair deep in thought, nods absently.*

Gottleb: We'll make him confess the truth. Fräulein Jost, Herr Cranach, concentrate there on his bald spot. There . . . Concentrate . . .

Cranach: No. I can't let one of my staff risk speaking the truth out loud in public.

Gottleb: It won't hurt him. He's amongst friends. Now concentrate . . . three Aryan minds converge . . . burn into his brain . . . h-a-r-d- . . . the truth . . .

> **Gottleb, Cranach** *and* **Else** *stare fixedly across at the top of* **Stroop***'s head. Jaws tighten, eyes bulge in the tense silence. Finally,* **Stroop** *opens his mouth and belches. They continue concentrating.* **Stroop** *suddenly clutches his head, lets out a low moan and rises unsteadily from his chair.*

Stroop: Clara Bow's panties. Willy Frisch and Lilian Harvey and the hair from Adolph Menjou's moustache. Oh, the glories of man's unconquerable past. Hans Albers' tights! His legs were too thin for him to play Hamlet, alas poor Yorick, one fool in the grave.

Cranach: ⎫
Gottleb: ⎬ Root it out. Root it out.
Else: ⎭

Stroop: No, it's the truth. It was different then. The sky never so blue, the snow never so white. I was remembering a

Christmas I spent in the country. Every house with evergreens decorated with stars. A man pulling a cart heaped with holly. A girl herding geese through a gate. A little boy listening at the bedroom door to the music and dancing below.

Else: When I was a girl, Mother used to take me to afternoon dances at the Vaterland. They hung the hall with Chinese lanterns in the summer and the girls were given posies of violets. Mother'd sit knitting and Father'd read the 'B.Z. Zum Mittag' and I danced to the music of 'Madam Jodl and Her All Ladies Viennese Orchestra.'

Lights down slightly. There is an illusion of swaying Chinese lanterns overhead as **Stroop** *bows to* **Else** *and dances her solemnly round the office whilst* **Cranach** *and* **Gottleb** *hum a Strauss waltz.*

Cranach: Our garden had carnations of all colours, nasturtiums, snap-dragons, Madonna lilies, monthly roses. Mother loved flowers so, she said they never tried to borrow money. How long the summers were then, how bright the sun. Smell the jasmine round the arbour walls.

Without stopping the dance, he takes **Stroop**'s *place as* **Else**'s *partner whilst* **Stroop** *hums with* **Gottleb**, *who is crying. The dance ends and* **Cranach** *escorts* **Else** *back to her desk.*

Gottleb: My mother was a saint. She was born to laugh; instead her whole life was spent crying and saying goodbye. My father ran off with a waitress. Three brothers killed West Front 1918, when we were stabbed in the back. She raised six, always telling me I had to sleep faster, she needed the pillows. Fifty years on her knees scrubbing for Jews and Bolsheviks. From a person to a nonentity, face worn to the bone. 'What's dying?' she asked. 'What I've had in life was worse.' Yet she was gentle as water, so good, birds perched on her outstretched hand. *(he sings, sobbing)* 'I see your eyes at sunset's golden hour. They look on me till night's first stars above. You speak to me across the silent land. From out the long ago, Mother I love . . .'

Gottleb's **Mother**, *a little old lady, head wrapped in a black shawl, hobbles on Wings Left.*

Gottleb's Mother: Son, son, I need food.

Gottleb: Mother, don't bother me now, can't you see I'm

singing. *(he sings)* 'I hold your hand as through the world I go. And think of your sweet face gentle as a little dove. Your presence fills each throbbing hour of life. Oh heart of long ago, Mother I love . . .'

Gottleb's Mother: But, son, I haven't eaten for three days.

Gottleb: Didn't I give you a new pair of shoes for your birthday?

Gottleb's Mother: Three days without food!

Gottleb: How did you get past the guard dogs? Mother, you climbed over the wall again. *(singing)* 'God keep your memory fragrant in my soul. And lift my eyes in thankfulness above. Until I stand beside you at the last. And hold you in my arms, Mother I love.'

Gottleb's Mother: Food! Food!

She turns and staggers off Wings Left. **Gottleb** *passes a hand over his eyes. Lights Full Up.*

Gottleb: Had no time for her then, the Party came first, last and always. Too old, too late to share it. But the song's true, the pain real, despite . . . *(he raises his glass)* My mother.

They all drink; as they pour another glass each, he sways over to **Cranach**.

I was wrong about you, Viktor, you've got Aryan qualities. So've you, Fräulein Else, and even you Heinz, or can I call you Stroop. *(he clasps* **Cranach***)* I need new friends, I keep eating up the old ones. Let's be friends.

Else: Why not? I've always found it easy to be friends with men I dislike physically.

Stroop: I haven't made any friends since I was in my forties, after I realised they couldn't save me.

Cranach: You're right, Gottleb — Hans. Friendship's a reciprocal conciliation of mutual interests. We're natural allies, dedicated to building the best. On the personal level too we've much in common. We both earn twenty thousand marks a week, only they don't pay us it. Without us, the machine grinds, halts, and it all spills out. *(they put their arms round each other)* Salt of the earth . . . brother in arms . . . have another drink.

Gottleb: We should've been friends before. I blame our Sturmbannführers. Towers of jelly, not a healthy fart amongst the lot of 'em. When we came to power I thought we'd build gold pissoirs in the streets. Instead they do it in their diapers. They run bowel-scared so they set Amt C against Amt D, D against B. The place is alive with hate-beetles. And Brigade-führer Gluck's the worst. Brigadeführer! He wouldn't make a first class doorman for a second class hotel, he's about as sharp as a billiard ball; why're my superiors always my inferiors? In the old days it was bow-legged turds with their University degrees and diplomas lording it; dead fish stinking from the head.

Cranach: Academics, the higher education breed, as useful as two left feet, trying to imagine what the flame of a candle looks like after it's been blown out. Never liked 'em.

Gottleb: Book-readers! They read *books*. We showed 'em books. Books is nothing! I've burnt ten thousand books in a night, reduced 'em to a pile of ash — well, they're easier to carry that way. Now we've got a new bunch of snot-pickers up there giving us orders. I can give orders 'stead of taking 'em. MARCH! SHOOT! DIE! Our day to crow it in the sun. MARCH! SHOOT! DIE! That was the promise and the dream. *(he pulls off his moustache)* We was robbed again. MARCH . . . SHOOT . . . DIE . . .

Stroop: I was ruined when I was twelve. I found a fifteen thousand mark note in the gutter and I spent the rest of my life with my eyes fixed on the ground, always looking down instead of ahead. If I could've seen where I was going it would've been different. I was young, strong, hard. They couldn't've stopped me. I'd've had a new uniform with bright buttons and boots up to the calf. Leather boots to step on fat faces, boots, boots, marching up and down again left-right, left-right, *crunch, craa* . . .

   He raises his rigid legs and smacks them down savagely as he 'goose-steps' frantically round the office until he ricks himself and has to hobble painfully back to his chair.

Else: For two thousand years Christians've worshipped the Cross and made women like me carry it. If I hadn't had a bad case of Catholic conscience, I could've been mistress of Silesia by now. When I was in the Ministry, Gauleiter Hanke wanted what I had. I said he couldn't have it, it was Lent. So he took a pimple-faced shop girl from the Wittenbergplatz. Prussian blockhead. His idea of style was mirrors in the bedrooms, fountains in the hall, and bull-necked SS men serving tea in white gloves. White gloves! Oh what taste and elegance I could've shown him.

She sweeps around, acknowledging imaginary guests with gracious smiles and nods.

A luxury villa in Dahlen, dining every night at the 'Horcher' or driving to the 'Furst von Stollberg' in the Harz Mountains. I could've set the tone for the best society. Instead we have Frau Goebbels rushing up to the wife of the Italian Minister, shouting 'Is that dress real silk?'

Stroop *(giggling)*: You know what Frau Emmy said to Reich-Marshal Goering at their wedding reception. 'Why've you got on your tuxedo and medals Herman, this isn't a first night.'

Else: She's given up membership of the Church, she's lost faith in the resurrection of the flesh.

They gather round laughing.

Cranach: Don't laugh. It's an offence to make people laugh. Jokes carry penalties. So don't. Have you tried the new Rippentrop herrings? They're just ordinary herrings with the brain removed and the mouth split wider.

Shrieks from **Else** *and* **Stroop,** *whilst* **Gottleb** *roars and slaps his thigh in delight. Their laughter quickly grows louder and more hysterical.*

Gottleb: That'll get you five years hard labour, Viktor. Here's one carries ten: my dentist is going out of business. Everyone's afraid to open their mouths.

Else: The only virgin left in Berlin is the angel on top of the victory column — Goebbels can't climb that high.

Gottleb: I sentence you to fifteen years, Fräulein.

Else: A German's dream of paradise is to have a suit made of genuine English wool with a genuine grease spot in it.

Gottleb: Another fifteen.

Stroop: We can't lose the war, we'd never be that careless.

Gottleb: Twenty years hard.

Stroop: The time we'll really be rid of the war is when Franco's widow stands beside Mussolini's grave asking who shot the

Führer?

Gottleb: Thirty.

Cranach: Listen, listen, what do you call someone who sticks his finger up the Führer's arse?!

Gottleb: Heroic.

Cranach: No, a brain surgeon!

Gottleb: That's DEATH.

> *Cranach,* **Else** *and* **Stroop** *collapse in hysterical laughter. But it dies away as they become aware that a suddenly sober* **Gottleb** *is staring balefully at them.*

Cranach: You're not laughing, Hans.

Gottleb: But I am inside, *inside. (he stamps round triumphantly)* I have you strung up and out, Cranach! I waited and I won it. You didn't realise I'm abnormally cunning, like most fanatics. Death's mandatory for all jokes, good or bad, about our beloved Führer-make-him-happy-he-deserves-it. No more talk of not giving Krupp AG that CP3 (m) contract. I'll have you in front of People's Court Judge Rehse, in a day, sentenced and hanging from piano wire by the end of the week. Job, family, life, lost in one, Cranach. And the rest of you're going under . . . 'His sacred arse . . . a finger up it . . . brain-surgeon.' Filthy! Filthy!

Cranach: Sacred arse . . . finger up . . . brain-surgeon? You've been drinking, Gottleb! I never tell jokes. Everyone knows I've no sense of humour.

Else: Nobody has in Amt C, the atmosphere isn't conducive.

Cranach: I know you want Krupps AG to get the CP(m) contract and us professional civil servants out. But you go too far in treating the Führer's arse – bless-it-and-make-it-happy-it-deserves-it as a joke. Every part of the Führer's super-human anatomy is treated with awesome respect in this office. We shout 'Heil Hitler, Heil Hitler, Heil Hitler' every morning. We worship him as a flawless being, a divinity, and you talk of his arse.

Gottleb: *I* don't, Cranach, *you* do . . .

> *The* **Others** *gasp and shake their heads in horror.*

Lies, shit-drizzle of lies. But I expected this.

> *He opens his brief-case, left on the desk and takes out a small tape-recording machine: the* **Others** *look puzzled.*

55

It's the latest example of Aryan technological genius. A magnetic tape-recording machine, just developed by Army Intelligence. A masterpiece of German ingenuity. The magnetization on the tape induces electrical currents in the coil, which are then amplified and reproduced, recreating the original sounds. Soon every home'll have one wired to a central control. Then every word spoken'll be noted and banked, no more secret words, only secret thoughts. And one day those too'll be taped. What a day that'll be. I switched it on when you started making jokes. You look ill Cranach, and you Stroop. I'll play it back, see if you think it's still funny. Somehow I don't think you'll laugh this time around, jokes've a way of dying too.

He starts to wind back the spools on the machine.

Stroop: I'm an old man, my legs don't bend so easy. I let the flies settle and the days burn out like matches. Herr Cranach did say something about arses and fingers. He said it, I didn't . . . I'm only repeating . . . you don't think I . . . how could . . . Heil Hitler! Heil Hitler!

Else: I heard Herr Cranach too. I'd have to swear it for my Mother's sake. She's a grand old lady over eighty now. Once met the Kaiser, more or less. I've been non-political for over thirty — twenty — years, so whoever it was it wasn't me! Heil Hitler! Heil Hitler!

Gottleb: I like it! I like it! I'm peeling you naked to the centre. I like it! I like it! Oh, I like it!

Cranach: I'm sure we all said things. I believe you even mentioned it'd be heroic touching up the Führer — MAKE-HIM-HAPPY-HE-DESERVES-IT. Bad schnapps talking, not a good German. We're all in this together.

Gottleb: Old lies, I shit on old lies. Here's something you'll hear beyond your death. The truth!

Cranach, Else and Stroop brace themselves. He switches on the tape-recorder to hear a cacophony of high-pitched screeches, muffled squawks and clicks. Cranach, Else and Stroop exchange looks, whilst Gottleb smiles complacently.

Gottleb: You can't lie your way out of that!

He leans closer to the recorder and repeats words only he can hear on the tape.

'What do you call someone who sticks his finger up the Führer's arse . . . ?' Disgusting! Disgusting . . . ! 'No, a brain-surgeon.' *(he switches off)* Ipso facto. Hang him.

Cranach: For what? It's just noise. Not one human voice. It doesn't work.

Gottleb: It doesn't work? The latest product of German technological genius and you say it doesn't work. That's anti-German slander. You could get another ten years on top of your death sentence for that. You don't hear anything because you don't want to. But I hear voices, clear as bells.

Cranach: That nobody else can hear. If you had more brains, Gottleb, you'd be in an asylum. Fräulein Jost, Herr Stroop, did you hear anything?

They both shake their heads. **Gottleb** *rewinds the spools.*

Gottleb: I'm not surprised. Women never listen, they haven't the glands and that old fool's half dead and completely stupid. But you can't get round hard facts. Listen.

He switches on the tape recorder again, which plays exactly the same noise.

NOW tell me you can't hear anything . . . ? 'Finger' . . . 'arse' . . . 'brain-surgeon' . . . The Gestapo'll take that as evidence. *(he switches off the recorder)* Especially when it's confirmed by your own staff. Fräulein Jost, Herr Stroop, you've already sworn he made the joke. Now it's your duty to swear his life away for the Fatherland. 1937 Civil Service Code, paragraph 6. No matter how humble his station in life, every German enjoys equal opportunity before the law, to denounce his social superiors. I appeal to your patriotism, or better still, your greed and envy. *(he rewinds the spools)* Remember informers inherit their victim's job as a reward.

He crosses and pours **Stroop** *a drink.*

Stroop, if you tell the truth and say you hear Cranach's voice on the tape, you take over his position. Think of it. Head of your own department at sixty-four. That's fantastic progress, for someone with your obvious limitations.

Stroop: Will I be able to sign memos, have the largest desk, two phones, lose my temper and no one have the right to answer back?

Gottleb: All yours, just tell the truth. *(pouring* **Else** *a drink)* And you Fräulein, from Acting Secretary Grade III (Admin) to Permanent Secretary Grade I with increased salary and pension, and permanent use of the first floor Grade I executive wash-rooms.

Else: I'm told each toilet seat's individually covered with an organdie doily, capped with a gilded swastika. Some women've stayed in those washrooms for days.

Gottleb: Shit-house decadence! It killed my father! But it's all yours if you tell the truth, hear Cranach's voice. Listen. LISTEN.

He switches on the recorder again and they listen hard.

Stroop: Yes . . . sounds behind the sounds . . . laughter . . . a voice.

Else: Faint . . . faint . . . what does it say?

Gottleb *(slowly)*: 'What do you call someone who sticks his finger up the Führer's arse?'

Else ⎱ *(repeating slowly)*: 'What do you call someone who
Stroop ⎰ sticks his finger up the Führer's arse?'

Gottleb: 'A brain-surgeon.'

Else ⎱ *(repeating slowly)*: 'A brain-surgeon.'
Stroop ⎰

There is a click. **Cranach** *has switched off the machine.*

Gottleb: Too late, Cranach. I've witnesses now. They heard. Who's guilty, Cranach? The punished man, the punished man!

He produces a children's Christmas toy squeaker and blows it repeatedly at **Cranach.**

Cranach: Fräulein, Herr Stroop, the joke's on you, not on the tape. Give him that finger and he'll want the whole hand.

He pours **Else** *and* **Stroop** *a drink from his bottle.*

Fräulein, he won't let you see a Grade I salary, pension or toilet seat. You're marked dead meat, cold water. And you, Heinz. You'll never become Department Head. It'll be Gottleb's thirty pieces reward for denouncing me. But he can only get it if you lie about me and the Führer's-make-him-happy-he-deserves-it famous arse. I know you won't lie. Over the years we three've formed an abiding relation, working together, grieving together when your wife died,

Heinz and your mother didn't, Fräulein. The best way to help ourselves is by helping each other. The times're sour, we've lost the true meaning of things, but I know I can still find integrity and trust amongst my friends.

Gottleb: 'Integrity', 'trust', 'friends.' Whenever I hear noble sentiments I reach for my wallet to see if it's been lifted. Your friends're selling you Cranach, because I can give 'em something better than 'integrity', 'trust', 'friendship'.

Cranach: So can I, Gottleb — 'security'. Fräulein, Herr Stroop, you measure out your days classifying, documenting, numbering. It's always the same, but always within your capabilities. Sometimes you're bored, but never anxious for you know tomorrow'll be the same as today. If you denounce me it'll never be the same again, only the same as outside, full of choice and change, violence and blood. Are you going to throw away all this security on the word of a man who every hour he's out of prison is away from home. He's not one of us. He isn't safe!

Else: No, Herr Cranach. I have to tell the truth. No matter who it hurts. A so-called joke about the location of the Führer's mighty brain-make-it-happy-it-deserves-it was told in this office.

Gottleb: Now it falls, it falls!

Else: By you, Herr Gottleb!

Stroop: You said he needed a finger-surgeon! We all heard you Gottleb. Filth! Filth!

Gottleb: He said it, I didn't . . . I was only repeating . . . you don't think I . . . how could . . . Heil Hitler . . . Wheezle-gutted, chicken-breasted vomit! In the old days every good German was an informer, now you can't rely on anyone to betray the right people. The true Aryan spirit's gone forever. I don't need white-livered, crow-bait.

Cranach: You do, Gottleb. Without them you've got nothing. *(he switches on the tape)* Nothing but laughter. They'll laugh you out, Gottleb, just as we're laughing you out.

Laughing loudly, Else, Stroop *and* Cranach *produce children's toy squeakers, put on Christmas paper hats and advance triumphantly on* Gottleb, *who defends himself by also putting on a paper hat and whipping out his toy squeaker. They blow furiously at each other. But* **Gottleb** *is outnumbered. He backs away, claps his hands over his ears and collapses in a chair.*

Cranach *switches off the recorder, whilst* **Else** *and* **Stroop** *continue jeering.* **Gottleb** *takes off his paper hat.*

Gottleb: I'm tired in advance. All these years fighting. The forces of reaction're too strong. Pulled down by blind moles in winged collars. Your kind can't be reformed, only obliterated. As you build 'em we should find room for you in one of our complexes in Upper Silesia: Birkenau, Monowitz or Auschwitz.

    Else *and* **Stroop** *stop jeering.*

That's where I should be too. Out in the field. Not stuck behind a desk in Orienburg, but in the gas-chambers of Auschwitz, working with people. Dealing with flesh and blood, not deadly abstractions: I'm suffocating in this limbo of paper. Auschwitz is where it's happening, where we exterminate the carrion hordes of racial maggots. I'd come into my own there on the Auschwitz ramp, making the only decision that matters, who lives, who dies. You're strong, live; you're pretty, live; you're too old, too weak, too young, too ugly. Die. Die. Die. Die. Smoke in the chimneys, ten thousand a week.

    Cranach, **Else** *and* **Stroop** *look disturbed.*

Stroop: What's he say? What's he say?

Cranach: Too much. Hold your tongue between your fingers, Gottleb, there're ladies present.

Else: I only type and file WVHA Amt C 1 (Building) to WVHA Amt D IV/5 your reference QZV/12/01 regulation E(5) PRV 24/6 DS 4591/1942.

Stroop: We only deal in concrete. We're Amt C 1 (Building). Test procedure 17 as specified structural work on outer surfaces of component CP3(m) described in regulation E(5), what's CP3(m) to do with life and death in Upper Silesia? Everybody knows I'm sixty-four years old.

Gottleb *(rising)*: You know extermination facilities were established in Auschwitz in June for the complete liquidation of all Jews in Europe. CP3(m) described in regulation E(5) is the new concrete flue for the crematoriums.

      Cranach, Else *and* Stroop *sit.*

Cranach: Who knows that?

Else **⎞**
         We don't know that.
Stroop **⎠**

Gottleb: You don't know that only knowing enough to know
    you don't want to know that. Future cases of death must be
    given consecutive Roman numbers with consecutive
    subsidiary Arabic numbers, Numerical I/1 to I/185. If you
    could see the dead roasted behind Roman numerals I/1 to
    Roman numeral XXX/185 you'd run chicken-shitless, but
    you haven't the imagination. Even if you read of six million
    dead, your imagination wouldn't frighten you, because it
    wouldn't make you see a single dead man. But I'll make you
    see six million! I'm going to split your minds to the sights,
    sounds and smells of Auschwitz. Then I'll be rid of you.
    You'll go of your own accord. You piss-legs haven't the
    pepper to stay in WVHA Amt C knowing every file you
    touch's packed tight with oven-stacked corpses. No way then
    to hide behind the words and symbols. You won't be able to
    glory in it like me, seeing the night trains halting at the ramp
    behind the entrance gate, between Birkenau and the
    Auschwitz parent camp. Don't you see the searchlights,
    guard dogs, watch towers, men with whips? And at the far
    end, Crematoria I and II, belching sticky-sweet smoke and
    waiting for the new concrete flues, CP3(m). Don't you see
    the trains carrying three thousand prisoners a time, eighty to
    a wagon built to hold thirty? They've been travelling five
    days without food or water so when the doors're open they
    throw the corpses out first, the sick fall next, stinking from
    typhus, diarrhoea, spotted fever. Hear the screaming?
    They're being beaten into lining up five abreast to march past
    the SS doctors. Those fit to work go right, those unfit, the
    old, sick, and young go to the left for gassing. Mothers try to
    hide their babes, but the Block Commanders always find
    'em. 'What's this shit?! This shit can't work!' They use the
    new-born babes as balls, kicking 'em along the ramp
    shouting 'Goal! Goal!'

Else *sobs,* **Stroop** *and* **Cranach** *cry out in protest as they clasp
    their heads in pain.*

You see! They're there, behind those files there, stripped, shaved, tattooed on their left arms 10767531. Two thousand living in block-houses, built for five hundred; primitive conditions for Europe's primitives. Work till you die, on a quarter loaf of bread and one bowl of soup made of potatoes, and old rags. Look there, see the labour gangs stagger out through the morning mists, to start their twelve-hour shift in Krupps' fuse factory, skin peeling back from their bones. No malingerers here, if sick, they're allowed one lick of an aspirin hanging on a string, two licks if they're really ill. Life expectancy four months. Some do survive and have to be killed off with benzine injections, dying, in those files, for being too strong or too weak. Amt C like Amt D's only concerned with dying. Dying by starvation, despair, crowbar, bullet, axe, meat-hook, surgeon's knife. Roman numerals LXX/27 to LXXXX/84, dying by chloral hydrate, phenol, evipan, air that kills, Roman numeral LLXI/30 to LLLXII/67. Trouble makers die hardest, hanging from window frames, hot radiators, see Roman numeral XXX/104; with iron clamps round temples; screwed tight, skulls craaaack, brains slurp out like porridge. 'Corpse carriers to the gate house at the double!'

Else, Cranach *and* **Stroop** *stagger up, shaking and moaning.*

We need more plants like Auschwitz, manufacturing and recycling dead Jews into fertilizing ash. We've already reached a peak output of 34,000 dead gassed and burned in one day and night shift. A record Belsen, Buchenwald, Dachau or Treblinka can't touch. And it's all due to the new gas chambers and crematoriums. You help build 'em so you should be able to see 'em plain. They've been made up to look like public bath houses. 'Our Wash and Steam'll Help You Dream.' The dressing rooms've signs in every European language, 'Beware of Pickpockets,' 'Tie Your Shoes Together and Fold Your Clothes,' 'The Management Take No Responsibility For any Losses Incurred.' Oh we're clever, we're clever. Don't you see how clever? It helps calm those marked down to die as they go naked along carpeted passages to the communal wash-room. Fifteen hundred a time.

There is the reverberating sound of a steel door shutting Up Stage. **Cranach, Stroop** *and* **Else** *whirl round to face it, clamping their hands over their ears.*

Now see, see 'em packed, buttock to buttock, gazing up at the waterless douches, wondering why the floor has no drainage runnels. On the lawns above, Sanitary Orderlies unscrew the lid shafts and Sergeant Moll shouts, 'Now let 'em eat it!' and they drop blue, Zyklon B hydro-cyanide crystals changing to gas in the air as it pours down and out through false shower heads, fake ventilators. What visions, what frenzies, the screaming, coughing, staggering, vomiting, bleeding, breath paralysed, lungs slowly ruptured *aaaaah!* See it! See it!

Twisting frantically to escape the sound of his voice, **Cranach, Else** *and* **Stroop** *gasp, cough and scream in panic.*

Children falling first, faces smashed against the concrete floor. Others tear at the walls hoping to escape. But see, they're falling too, flies in winter, rushing to the door, shrieking 'Don't let me die! Don't let me die! Don't let me die!', the strongest stamping the weakest down, all falling still, at last, a solid pyramid of dead flesh jammed against the wash-house door, limbs tied in knots, faces blotched, hands clutching hanks of hair, carcasses slimy with fear, shit, urine, menstrual blood they couldn't hold back. You see it now! Look! There! There!

Cranach: ⎱
Else: ⎰ We don't see! We don't see!
Stroop: ⎰

Gottleb *(pointing Up Stage)*: LOOK. Mind splits, death-house door slides open . . . SEE.

As the sound of the gas-chamber door being opened reverberates, the whole of the filing section Up Stage slowly splits and its two parts slide Up Stage Left, and Up Stage Right to reveal Up Stage Centre, a vast mound of filthy, wet straw dummies; vapour, the remains of the gas, still hangs about them. They spill forward to show all are painted light blue, have no faces, and numbers tattooed on their left arms.

Cranach, Stroop *and* **Else** *stare in horror and* **Gottleb** *smiles* *as two monstrous figures appear out of the vapour, dressed in black rubber suits, thigh-length waders and gas-masks. Each has a large iron hook, knife, pincers and a small sack hanging from his belt. As they clump forward, they hit the dummies with thick wooden clubs. Each time they do so there is the splintering sound of a skull being smashed.*

Gottleb: The Jewish Sonderkommando Sanitation Squad. They go in after, to see no-one's left alive and prepare the bodies for the fire ovens.

Slipping and sliding, the **Sanitation Men** *use their iron hooks to separate the dummies.*

They have to work fast, there's always another train-load waiting. *Faster! Faster!* New Sanitation Squads are brought in every three months and the old ones're sent to the ovens, all used up. *Faster! Faster!* Part of their job is to recover strategic war material for the Reich.

The **First Sanitation Man** *starts tearing at the mouth of a dummy with his pincers, accompanied by a loud, wrenching sound.*

Gold teeth. They're extracting gold teeth from the corpses. That's why they're called the 'Gold-diggers of 1942.' Root it out. Root it out! . . . Quicker, don't take half the jaw bone!

Whilst the **First Sanitation Man** *mimes putting the teeth into his sack, the* **Second Sanitation Man** *gouges a dummy's face with his knife.*

Glass eyes. This way we've thousands of spare glass eyes ready for empty German sockets. *Faster scum, you want to join the others in the fire pits?!*

The **First Sanitation Man** *quickly cuts off a dummy's finger and puts it in his sack.*

That's better. It saves time when you're collecting wedding rings to slice off the whole finger. *Faster scum! Faster! The ovens! The ovens! More coming. More coming.* SEE. See what's behind your files?!

As the **Sanitation Men** *rip, slice and gouge with increasing frenzy amid the noise of breaking bones and tearing flesh,* **Cranach, Else** *and* **Stroop** *jerk their heads from side to side and whirl around to avoid looking Up Stage.*

Cranach: I see it! I can't fight 'em. I couldn't say 'no' to them.

This isn't the time to say 'no'. I've just taken out a second mortgage!

Else: I see it too! But what can I do? I'm only one woman. How can I say 'no'? This isn't a good time for me either to say 'no'. Mother's just bought a new suite of furniture!

Stroop: Yes, I see it! But they'll stop me growing roses, wearing slippers all day. I'm peeing down my trouser leg. I'm an old man. You can't expect me to say 'no'. I couldn't say 'no', how can I say 'no' to them? It's a bad time to say 'no'. I'm retiring next year. I'd lose my gold watch!

Gottleb: *Faster garbage! Faster!*

Using their iron hooks, the **Sanitation Men** *stack the torn dummies in neat piles.*

They're laying out the meat for the fire-ovens. It's baking time. That's a sight you must see, see, see!

The **Others** *fall on their knees, facing Down Stage.*

4,500,000 killed and roasted. You'll smell 'em every morning you come into the office, crisp flesh done to a turn, all senses confirm, feathers torn from the wing.

Else *covers her eyes,* **Stroop** *his ears,* **Cranach** *his mouth.*

You'll find it hell 'less you get the hell out. So run. Hide. Find somewhere to hide. The sky's falling. This is men's work. *Faster! Faster!*

He moves Up Stage, yelling at the **Sanitation Men.** **Cranach** *takes his hands from his mouth.*

Cranach: Fight. Fight. Can't let him win. We're Civil Servants, words on paper, not pictures in the mind, memo AS/7/42 reference SR 273/849/6. Writers write, builders build, potters potter, book-keepers keep books. E(5) Class 1 and II, L11, L12, F280/515 your reference AMN 23D/7. 'Gas-chambers', 'fire-ovens', 'ramps', he's using words to make us see images, words to create meanings, not contained in them; then nothing means what it says and our world dissolves. Words're tools. CP(3)m is CP(3)m. Two capitals, a bracket round an Arabic numeral and a small letter 'm', the rest is the schnapps talking. 4,500,000 dead, no yardstick to measure, one four, one five, six noughts, brain can't encompass. *(he gets up)* Memo Amt C1 (Building) to Amt D1 (Central Office). Your reference EC2Z 5LZ. Our reference F68. We merely operate policies embodied in existing legislation and implement decisions of higher authority. Copies to Amt A (military administration) Amt B (military economy) Amt W (SS economic enterprises) . . .

He helps **Else** *and* **Stroop** *up.*

Get up, horizontal positions diminish the genius of the German people, we must always be vertical and hierarchical. It's all in the mind. He was lying. I could tell, he used *adjectives*. We merely administer camps which concentrate people from all over Europe. Are we going to let the wet dreams of an obscene buffoon like Gottleb drive us out? He said it, it's all imagination, and hard facts leave nothing to the imagination. We're trained to kill imagination before it kills us. So close mind's door, shut out the light there. Concentrate on what's real, what's concrete. Concentrate and repeat: Component CP(3)m, described in regulation E(5) serving as Class I or Class II appliance shall be so constructed as to comply with relevant requirements of regulations L2(4) and (6) L8(4) and (7).

Else: Component CP(3)m described in regulation E(5)
Stroop: serving as Class I or Class II appliance shall be so constructed as to comply with relevant requirements of regulation L2(4) and (6) L8(4) and (7) . . .

The steel door of the gas chamber is heard slowly closing and the two sections of filing cabinet Up Stage Left and Right begin to slide back into position Up Stage Centre, blocking off the dummies and the **Sanitation Men**. **Gottleb** *rushes back down to* **Cranach**, **Else** *and* **Stroop**.

Gottleb: You can't shut it out, not word play, dream play, I've been there! It's *real!*

Cranach: *(chanting):* Future cases of death shall be given
Else: consecutive Roman numbers with consecutive
Stroop: subsidiary Arabic numbers. The first case Roman numeral I/1 the second Roman numeral I/2 up to Roman numeral I/185. Thereafter the cases shall be numbered Roman numeral II from Roman numeral II/1 to Roman numeral II/185 . . .

The steel door is heard shutting with a final clang as the two filing sections are rejoined in their previous position, Up

*Stage. The **dummies** and **Sanitation Men** have vanished from sight behind them.*

Else: Sanctus, Sanctus, Sanctus. Benedictus Deus!

Stroop: All gone 'phoof', nothing disturbing left. It's a triumph.

Gottleb: Of mongoloid reasoning, I'll take you there . . . !

    Cranach *picks up* **Gottleb**'*s briefcase,* **Else** *his file and* **Stroop**, *whilst quickly finishing the last dregs, his schnapps bottle. They thrust them at him.*

Else: Knowing you Herr Gottleb makes it hard to believe all souls're equal in the sight of the Lord. Go break a leg.

Stroop: Drown yourself, it's funnier.

Cranach: Krupps AG won't get that contract in Upper Silesia and you won't get us out of Amt C. You're a man with both feet on the ground Gottleb, until they hang you; I'll send you a rope with instruction. You're OUT.

Gottleb: The final degradation, these old Party hairs, pissed on by secret Semites, obvious mediocrities. That's what's finally spoiled National Socialism for me, having to share it with people whose lack of imagination would diminish the Colosseum and the Taj Mahal by moonlight. I'd rather be a bad winner than any kind of loser. I can stand anything but defeat!

Cranach:
Else: }   Root it out!
Stroop:

    Gottleb *gives a yell as* **Else** *opens the door.* **Cranach** *and* **Stroop** *grab his arms and throw him out. As he lands in the corridor with a crash,* **Else** *slams the door shut. The three grin delightedly and congratulate each other.*

Else: I'll put in a RLS/47/3 to E6 (Cleaning and Maintenance) to have this office fumigated.

Cranach: Give it priority. Now perhaps we can get back to work. There's still a war to win.

    As they move back to their desk the door suddenly opens and **Gottleb** *pops his head in.*

Gottleb: I've still one more throw, the best and the last.

    He deliberately sticks his Hitler moustache back on his upper lip.

HAAA. Top that!

Before anyone can react, he quickly withdraws. **Cranach, Else** *and* **Stroop** *resume work.*

Stroop: That man could've done terrible things, overrode recognised procedures, ignored official channels, created precedents. You saved the department, Herr Cranach. I'm proud to've been able to help.

Else: We may not be much, but we're better than Gottleb. This time it didn't end with the worst in human nature triumphant, meanness exalted, goodness mocked. The other side has its victories. It's a Christmas present we'll remember, thanks to you, Herr Cranach.

Cranach: Thank you, Fräulein. In centuries to come when our complexes at Auschwitz're empty ruins, monuments to a past civilisation, tourist attractions, they'll ask, like we do of the Inca temples, what kind of men built and maintained these extraordinary structures. They'll find it hard to believe they weren't heroic visionaries, mighty rulers, but ordinary people, people who liked people, people like them, you, me, us.

Else *and* **Stroop** *look at him, then all three march Down Stage to sing at the audience with increasing savagery.*

Cranach ⎫ *(singing):* 'This is a brotherhood of man A benevolent
Else ⎬ brotherhood of man. A noble tie that binds, all
Stroop ⎭ human hearts and minds. Into a brotherhood of man. Your life-long membership is free. Keep a-giving each brother all you can. Oh aren't you proud to be in that fraternity. The great big brotherhood of man.' Sing! Everybody sing!

Lights go down and an unseen chorus joins the finale in the darkness.

EPILOGUE

Announcer's Voice: Stop. Don't leave. The best is yet to come. Our final number. The Prisoners Advisory Committee of Block B, Auschwitz II, proudly present as the climax of this Extermination Camp Christmas Concert, the farewell appearance of the Boffo Boys of Birkenau, Abe Bimko and Hymie Bieberstein — 'Bimko and Bieberstein!'

Introductory music. Applause. A Follow Spot picks out two hollow-eyed comics, **Bimko** *and* **Bieberstein** *as they enter dancing, Stage Right, dressed in shapeless concentration camp, striped prison uniforms with the yellow Star of David pinned on their threadbare tunics, wooden clogs, and undertakers top hats complete with ribbon. Carrying a small cane each, they perform a simple dance and patter routine, to the tune of 'On the Sunny Side of the Street'.*

Bieberstein: Bernie Litvinoff just died.

Bimko: Well if he had a chance to better himself.

Bieberstein: Drunk a whole bottle of varnish. Awful sight, but a beautiful finish. Everyone knew he was dead. He didn't move when they kicked him. He's already in the ovens.

Bimko: Poke him up then, this is a very cold block house.

Bieberstein: They're sending his ashes to his widow. She's going to keep them in an hour-glass.

Bimko: So she's finally getting him to work for a living.

Bieberstein: The Campo Foreman kept hitting me with a rubber truncheon yesterday — *hit, hit, hit.* I said, 'You hitting me for a joke or on purpose?' 'On purpose!' he yelled. *Hit, hit, hit.* 'Good,' I said, 'because such jokes I don't like.'

Bimko: According to the latest statistics, one man dies in this camp everytime I breathe.

Bieberstein: Have you tried toothpaste?

Bimko: No, the Dental Officer said my teeth were fine, only the gums have to come out.

Bieberstein: Be grateful. The doctor told Fleischmann he needed to lose ten pounds of ugly fat, so they cut off his head.

The music has faded out imperceptibly into a hissing sound. The Follow Spot begins to turn blue. They stop dancing.

Bimko: I'm sure I've got leprosy.

Bieberstein: Devil's Island's the place for leprosy.

Bimko: It's good?

Bieberstein: It's where I got mine.

Bimko: Can I stay and watch you rot?

They cough and stagger.

Bieberstein: I could be wrong but I think this act is dying.

Bimko: The way to beat hydro-cyanide gas is by holding your breath for five minutes. It's just a question of mind over matter. They don't mind and we don't matter.

They fall to their knees.

Bieberstein: Those foul, polluted German bastardized . . .

Bimko: Hymie, Hymie, please; what you want to do — cause trouble?

They collapse on the floor, gasping.

Bieberstein: To my beloved wife Rachel I leave my Swiss bank account. To my son Julius who I love and cherish, like he was my son, I leave my business. To my daughter I leave one hundred thousand marks in Trust. And to my no-good brother-in-law Louie who said I'd never remember him in my will — Hello Louie!

Bimko: Dear Lord God, you help strangers so why shouldn't you help us? We're the chosen people.

Bieberstein: Abe, so what did we have to do to be chosen?

Bimko: Do me a favour, don't ask. Whatever it was it was too much . . . Hymie you were right, this act's dead on its feet.

The Spot fades out.

Bieberstein: Oh mother . . .

They die in darkness.

THE END

Acknowledgement
Lines from *The Brotherhood of Man* are reproduced by kind permission of Frank Music Corporation, 1350 Avenue of the Americas, New York.

70

DATE DUE

MP 728